Happiness Here and Now

Elizabeth West

Happiness Here and Now

THE EIGHTFOLD PATH

OF JESUS

Revisited with Buddhist Insights

A MEDIO MEDIA BOOK

CONTINUUM

NEW YORK   LONDON

2000

The Continuum International Publishing Group Inc
370 Lexington Avenue, New York, NY 10017

The Continuum International Publishing Group Ltd
Wellington House, 125 Strand, London WC2R OBB

Printed in the United States of America

Library of Congress Cataloging-in-Publication Data

West, Elizabeth.
    Happiness here and now : the eightfold path of Jesus : revisited with
Buddhist insights / by Elizabeth West.
        p. cm.
    ISBN 0-8265-1245-9
    1. Beatitudes.   2. Spiritual life—Christianity.   3. Christianity and
other religions—Buddhism.   4. Eightfold Path.   5. Spiritual life—
Buddhism.   6. Buddhism—Relations—Christianity.   I. Title.

BT382.W47 2000
241.5'3—dc21

                                                                99-056795

To

HIS HOLINESS THE DALAI LAMA

*in gratitude for the time he has given to
dialogue with Christians. May the friendship
between Buddhism and Christianity flourish in
the future.*

Contents

Acknowledgments

I wish to thank all my Buddhist friends, too numerous to mention, in various traditions, who have been so open and generous in sharing their experience and teachings with me as a Christian. Special thanks to Thanissara and Kittisaro, Ajahn Candasiri from Amaravati and the Thai forest tradition, and Sister Annabel Laity of Plum Village, who have been partners in leading Buddhist-Christian retreats. Thanks too to Rigpa and Jamyang Tibetan Centres for their friendship and support in the work of dialogue. Special thanks to Father Laurence Freeman, OSB, and the Christian Meditation community in London for their support and guidance.

Christian Foreword

Ideas of happiness, like those about beauty, may vary from one culture to another but the experience is universally recognizable. Human happiness looks and feels the same everywhere. As it is one of the great universals, it is not surprising that all the great wisdom traditions have a teaching about happiness which takes us both to the particular heart of each religion as well as to the essential unity of vision they share.

The Christian idea of happiness is epitomized in the Beatitudes found in Jesus' great Sermon on the Mount. The teaching that happiness is found through poverty, hunger, and suffering transformed by spiritual vision, not through the crude satisfaction of desire, places this sermon in immediate relationship with the Buddha's great Sermon in the Deer Park. By understanding happiness and understanding how we understand it, we can thus grow in profound understanding of each others' seed traditions. Friendship grows from understanding. Peace is the flower of friendship.

Elizabeth West enters bravely into this process in this book. She looks from a Christian perspective at the way a Buddhist, whose perspective she has a deep empathy with, can look at the Beatitudes. Learning to see the familiar with freshness and new wonder is to expand our minds and enrich our hearts. New perspectives deepen insight. Reading her book with an openness to these different—but mutually re-inforcing—points of view helps one better to enter into the great spiritual project that lies ahead

Laurence Freeman, OSB
World Community for Christian Meditation

Buddhist Foreword

It was several years between the time I was first invited to teach a Christian-Buddhist retreat with Elizabeth and our first retreat together. Twice, during that time I was invited, but nothing actually happened. On each occasion my inner response was one of relief. By the third time it seemed I was ready—ready to open to teachings and a Path that I had turned aside from some twenty years previously. In 1996, Elizabeth and I accepted Father Roger Bacon's invitation to co-lead our first Christian-Buddhist retreat at Worth Abbey.

Although we had met before and Elizabeth had already had some experience of guiding such retreats, I was grateful that she took time to visit me at Chithurst Monastery before the retreat. This enabled us to consider ways of creating a structure within which to share silence and teachings from our respective traditions. More importantly, it provided an opportunity for a sense of spiritual kinship to arise between us; this in turn nourished a strong sense of friendliness and community among those who gathered with us for those days of retreat. It allowed us to transcend any differences on the level of personality or belief, and to meet at the level of the heart—of our shared humanity.

When I had first made a commitment to living within a Buddhist contemplative order, it felt very much like "the next step" on a path towards wholeness, towards an easeful relationship with myself and others. True, it might seem a very long way from the teachings of the Episcopal Church with which I grew up, but I was struck by the fact that much of the guidance I received at that time, far from conflicting with the teachings of Jesus Christ, actually confirmed them. It seemed to me that Jesus and the Buddha were pointing to the same Truth, and the same practices of relinquishment necessary for the realisation of that Truth. In a sense, this should not come as a surprise since both of these remarkable teachers had seen into the nature of existence; each in his own way was pointing to a path leading to perfect wholeness, or freedom, that accorded with this realisation. Ajahn Chah, our teacher from the Thai Forest Tradition, once said when questioned about the nature of Ultimate Reality: "There can only be one Ultimate Reality. You can't have a Buddhist Ultimate Reality that is different from Christian Ultimate Reality." What is different are the historical and cultural contexts in which the teachings were given, and the structures that have evolved to support us on our journey towards that Truth.

However, it is not a small thing to actually open to another religion. Perhaps in the hearts of some people there might be a fear that if they open themselves to the teachings of another faith they will become at best confused, at worst (as happened to me) "hooked," unable to turn back. In this book Elizabeth asks people to take that risk—as she herself has done. As with Christian-Buddhist retreats, this approach would seem to be most fruitful for people who already have a strong commitment to practice within their own tradition.

It can enhance, and even challenge, their own understanding without threatening it as might happen in the case of those whose faith and practice are less firmly established.

So we have here an invitation to enter into a process of guided contemplation. Each chapter is a presentation of Jesus' teachings on the Way to True Happiness. Pointers given by the Lord Buddha further illuminate these teachings, which indicate some of the most easily discernible, yet easily overlooked facts of our human existence. Each chapter ends with reflections and exercises designed to help us apply these teachings to our own situation, thereby allowing them to take root in our lives. So with even the most cursory glance at any one of these pages, we are provoked: "Wake up! What does this really mean? Might Jesus have intended this?" And we are also given the freedom to form our own opinions. While we may agree or disagree with what is surmised, it would be difficult to dismiss it altogether, to pass by without some consideration. It would also be an important opportunity missed for enriching our own spiritual life and understanding.

In conclusion, I would like to mention something that I have found important to keep in mind in my own spiritual practice, which is that both Jesus Christ and the Lord Buddha shared what they knew for the welfare and happiness of human beings. They were not trying to catch us out, humiliate or make us feel guilty; it is we who, all too readily, do this to ourselves when we first glimpse our human pain and limitation. Instead, this book encourages us to face that suffering, to acknowledge it as it is, without either excusing ourselves or exaggerating the problem. We are guided to an appreciation that it is only through full acceptance of suffering that we can transcend it; it is only through crucifixion that there can be resurrection.

Ajahn Candasiri
Amaravati Buddhist Monastery

Preface

This book has grown out of my own experience. My study and practice in the Buddhist tradition has deepened and enriched my Christian faith. When we enter into deep dialogue with another faith, the result is invariably that our own faith is both changed and deepened. The dialogue of practice is even more demanding in this respect than the dialogue of ideas. We can exchange ideas without being deeply affected ourselves; sharing practice leads to deeper levels which cannot be entered without letting go both of fear and prejudice on the one hand, and attachment to concepts on the other.

Participating in the leadership of Buddhist-Christian retreats has allowed me to see just how wonderfully this type of exchange can enrich our faith and practice. This book is intended to enable the reader to enter into such an experience. It can be used in time of retreat, or for daily reflection. It will lead the reader into an experience of Christ's teaching as a practical way to personal transformation. Buddhist insights show the Beatitudes as a path to salvation/liberation.

Sometimes we fail to see the Gospels as practical teachings on how to live and grow and change. When being taught from the pulpit Christianity may be presented in such a way that people are left feeling that they know well what they ought to do and be, but experience little help as to how to do it. This can be particularly true when it comes to teaching on prayer. This book is meant to help to address this need and enable the reader to see both what needs to change in them and how to enable that change to take place.

In the course of leading retreats I have discovered many people living in the borderland between Buddhism and Christianity. Some do this with ease; others struggle for a deeper sense of integration. Many have learned to meditate in the Buddhist tradition because they believed nothing of that nature existed in Christianity. Discovering Christian meditation enables them to look again at their own roots. I hope that this book will be a support to all those who find themselves in this borderland for one reason or another, as well as a door for those wishing to deepen their faith through dialogue.

Introduction

The purpose of this book is to provide the reader with a means of exploring the transforming power of deep dialogue.[1] Above all this book is about *practice* not about theory. It is meant as a tool in the hand of the reader to foster personal growth in mind, body, and spirit. It offers a way of opening the mind and heart to deeper understanding of religious traditions as ways of transformation.

The means used for this purpose is a journey of *lectio divina*.[2] The text to be explored is Matthew 5:1–10, the sayings of Jesus know as the Beatitudes. The reflection on the text will use insights from the teachings of the Buddha to bring out new layers of understanding for the reader. This will then be followed, after each chapter, by a practical exercise. The purpose of these exercises is to bring the application of the teaching into the life of the reader and so enhance growth and change in response to the teachings contained within each Beatitude. Meditation is the underpinning practice that will enable the best use of the text.

[1] The dialogue between religious traditions at the level of practice and experience rather than belief and doctrine.
[2] Contemplative reading of Scripture. This form of slow reflective reading has been practiced in Christian monasteries for hundreds of years, and it leads the reader into a deep personal relationship with the text which enhances self-knowledge and insight.

Before beginning the reflection on the Beatitudes, the means of reflection need to be understood. Thus the first few chapters of the book will be given to this purpose.

The first chapter will explore the meaning of interfaith dialogue and offer an opportunity for you to reflect on your personal response and attitudes to this dialogue. Dialogue is a multilevel activity. In this book you are being taken into the deepest level of dialogue. At this level one tradition enlightens the teaching of another to foster the personal growth of the participants.

The second chapter will explain the process of meditation as a way of contemplative prayer for the Christian. Meditation is a universal practice found in all traditions. It is the journey beyond words to direct experience and therefore automatically includes self-knowledge and growth. Words can avoid change; direct experience brings one face to face with the need for growth and progress towards wholeness.

The third chapter will explore the relationship between meditation and psychology by way of preparation for seeing the Beatitudes in the light of both.

Chapter four lays out the Beatitudes alongside the Buddha's Eightfold Noble Path and shows how they are both maps for life's journey, each in their own different ways. Readers who have no knowledge of Buddhism are recommended to read the appendix, which gives a brief overview of Buddhism, before proceeding.

There are a variety of ways in which this book could be used. I do not recommend that it be read from cover to cover as a theoretical or story book would be. It could be most fruitfully used as an aid to a time of retreat, using one Beatitude and reflection for each day of the retreat, or one beatitude per month for a day of retreat and life reflection. However you choose to use it, I strongly recommend that you give adequate time to each Beatitude, working with the exercises following each chapter. In this way it can lead to a deepened understanding of life as a spiritual journey to wholeness and unity with the divine, which is the destiny of every human person.

Happiness Here and Now

Chapter 1

Interfaith Dialogue

I n this century the religions of the world have come together as never before. For centuries the major world
religions flourished in their own parts of the world and rarely
came face to face. In the age of the modern empires of the
West, Christian missionaries carried Christianity to all parts
of the World. Members of other religions were seen as potential converts. There were few attempts at dialogue and
the institutional church quickly condemned them.[3] In this
atmosphere each religion remained a world unto itself.
Christianity was often in conflict with other faiths, the worst
example of which was the Crusades.

Towards the end of the last century all this began to
change. With the first Parliament of Religions held in Chi-
cago in 1898, and the famous address that Swami Vivek-
ananda gave there, the movement of the eastern religions
into the West had begun. The migrations of peoples over
the last hundred years have turned this early trickle into a
flood. In the sixties the tide began to flow in the other direction with more and more young people going East in
search of wisdom. Today this mingling of religions is a fact
of life and generally attitudes have radically changed.

[3]Matteo Ricci in China and Robert de Nobili in India, both Jesuits, are
examples of such attempts. However in their explorations and incultur-
ation conversion was always their goal.

During the Second Vatican Council the Spirit led the Roman Catholic Church to a major change of attitude to other religions, which really began the movement of interfaith dialogue. There were pioneers and visionaries preparing the way for this change of heart, but they had been voices crying in the wilderness. Then almost overnight they became the voices of the church for the future. The Council Fathers wrote the following:

> The Catholic Church rejects nothing of what is true and holy in other religions. She has a high regard for the manner of life and conduct, the precepts and doctrines, which although differing in many ways from her own teaching, nevertheless often reflect a ray of that truth which enlightens all people. . . . The Church therefore, urges her members to enter with prudence and charity into discussion and collaboration with members of other religions. Let Christians while witnessing to their own faith and way of life, acknowledge, preserve and encourage the spiritual and moral truths found among non-Christians, also their social life and culture.[4]

Although today this may sound patronizing, it is still a revolutionary statement, marking a new era in the history of Christianity. Many Catholics have not yet awoken to the full implications of this statement. The interfaith work of this present pope has been most important. The meeting of the leaders of the religions in Assisi to pray for peace in 1986 was surely a groundbreaking event.

Today, in countries like the U.K. and the U.S.A., where

4Vatican Council II, *Nostra Aetate*, ed. Austin Flannery (1981), 739.

representatives of all the religions of the world live and work side by side, all the major Christian denominations are aware of the need for interfaith dialogue and have made their own statements and issued guidelines for dialogue.[5] It has become an essential element in the search for world peace and social harmony.

From this brief summary it is clear that interfaith dialogue is here to stay and will become an ever more important issue in the next millennium. For the Catholic Church the pope continues to see dialogue as of major importance for the next millennium, as many of his recent statements indicate.[6]

There are several types of dialogue, all of which have their place. I will outline them briefly:

1. *Educational Dialogue*: this is particularly important in multicultural areas, where neighbours may be people of another faith and culture. It fosters tolerance and understanding. Through meeting and visiting places of worship other than one's own, respect and appreciation can replace fear and antagonism. Even in areas which are not yet mixed good educational and integrative programs can create tolerance. Religious tolerance is an essential ingredient in world peace, so this level is of great importance for the next millennium. Multifaith education in schools in an important part of this aspect.

2. *Intellectual Dialogue*: this is more for the academic world where experts in aspects of their own religion come to-

---

[5]*In Good Faith: The Four Principles of Dialogue. A Brief Guide for the Churches* (CCBI Inter-Church House). *Other Faiths: What Does the Church Teach* (CTS Pamphlet).
[6]*Fides et Ratio* (Faith and Reason) 1998.

gether to discuss and debate issues. When well done this can do much to develop new approaches to theology and philosophy for all traditions. It helps to deepen our awareness of the common ground and to value differences.

3. *Dialogue of Service*: where communities of different faith join together for social action, aid projects, pastoral care, work for peace, and help for refugees, etc. In the UK there has been progress on this level in working for joint chaplaincies in hospitals and universities, in working for refugees and asylum seekers.[7]

4. *Dialogue of Worship*: exploring ways people of different faith can pray and worship together. This is the newest and probably the most difficult area. Worship at civic occasions and interfaith marriages would be examples of this.

5. *Dialogue of Silence*: this type of dialogue is central to the growth of deep dialogue where people can explore without fear both the common ground and the differences between their faiths. When people have meditated together and touched the realm of unity beyond words, the words and structures which can divide us take their rightful place in the hierarchy of values and cease to be threatening, but instead are sources of richness. Interfaith retreats would be an example of this type of dialogue. The content of this book is an exercise in this. From dialogue through keeping silence together, the sharing of ways of practice becomes possible and mutually beneficial.

[7]In the U.K. an Interfaith Network has been founded to be a forum where issues of importance to any faith in Britain can be addressed, and such issues can be brought to public notice and promoted as required.

The Christian churches cautiously encourage all these forms of dialogue in varying degrees. The dialogue between Buddhism and Christianity is the most widespread and well developed, particularly on the spiritual level. The dialogue with Islam on the other hand tends to be more political and social and to leave religious issues aside, agreeing to differ. An important reason for the level of spiritual sharing between Buddhism and Christianity is the large numbers of westerners who are converting to Buddhism.

To enter into dialogue at any level certain attitudes are essential:

1. *Respect*: to approach the faith of someone else it is essential to "take off our shoes" and remember that where we tread is holy ground and that the Holy Spirit has no favorites— and was there before us! Faith is a deeply personal thing, and it is important to withhold judgment and negative criticism at least until we have walked a mile in their moccasins!

2. *Openness*: people will detect at once if they sense any superiority or lack of interest in our approach to them. It is important to recognise that we have much to learn from others before we can teach them anything.

3. *Adaptability and sensitivity*: to abide by the rules and regulations of another faith when we are on their territory is essential. Thus it is important to be very observant especially if we are not sure what the requirements are.

4. *No proselytizing*: The desire to convert or convince another is destructive of dialogue. It is very important to remember that Christians have a reputation for proselytising and pressurising others. Hence they are often suspected of having conversion as their motive in dialogue, thus it

is important to show true humility and willingness to value and learn from the other.

5. *Courage*: the journey of dialogue changes a person, so if you do not want to face the challenges it presents, better not to begin. Above all, much to the surprise of many people, dialogue will deepen and enrich your own faith rather than diminish it as many fear. This is the purpose of this book: to lead the reader on such a journey of depth and discovery. This could be the case whatever the faith background of the reader.

Nonduality—Learning from the Wisdom of the East

At their deepest level all major religious traditions have a nondual understanding of God. This usually expresses itself in the mystical teaching of each religion. Father Bede Griffiths pointed this out by his very simple illustration of the hand.[8] At the tips of the fingers, which represent the external forms of religion, the different religions appear to be far apart as do the fingers and thumb. But when you follow them to their root in the palm of the hand, there they all merge into a single source and unite. This points to the ultimate unity of all religions in the Divine Source, which we call God.

Traditionally in the study of world religions scholars tend to divide religions into theistic and nontheistic or monotheistic, polytheistic and monistic. Personally I think these terms are misleading and sometimes appear to imply nega-

---

[8]*The Human Search*, produced by More Than Illusions Pictures. A video of the life of Bede Griffiths, it is obtainable from Medio Media Ltd in the U.K.

tive judgment of the other. What these terms signify is that there are basically two branches of religions. Those that have grown out of the Jewish tradition and those that have grown out of what we have called Hinduism.

Thus we have:

a) The Semitic Religions—Judaism, Christianity, Islam and the Baha'i Faith.

b) The Eastern Religions—Hinduism, Buddhism, Jainism, Sikhism.

c) Zoroastrianism, the ancient religion of Persia, which now mainly exists in India, is between the two and had some influence on the Semitic as well as the Asian religions. The Wise Men in the nativity story may well have been Zoroastrians.

The Semitic religions have always been inclined to dualistic expression, although a growth in the understanding of God leads to nondual expressions at the mystical level of these faiths. The Kabalists and the Sufis, the mystical traditions of Judaism and Islam respectively both reach into the nondual reality. However writers such as Neil Douglas-Klotz maintain that the languages of the Middle East give a much more nondual vision of God and the world than these teachings have when translated into Greek and modern Western languages.

It is certainly clear that the Semitic religions have a much more personal view of God, which often has an anthropomorphic flavor, whereas the Asian religions see God more in terms of energies, ground of being, ocean of existence, etc. In Hinduism the incarnations and/or lesser deities fulfil the need for a personal God.

This is a simple and brief attempt to give a glimpse of a very profound and complex subject.

Where does Christianity stand in all this? The teaching of Christianity often appears dualistic in its approach. Mystics have often been regarded with suspicion and many, including John of the Cross and Teresa of Ávila, barely escaped the inquisition by cloaking their experiences in language acceptable to the church authorities. Meister Eckhart is the Western Christian mystic who comes closest to the Eastern traditions. Although condemned in his time he has since been reinstated and recognised as an important mystical theologian. He speaks of the Godhead beyond the Trinity.

When the Gospels are read in the light of such eastern scriptures as the Upanishads and the Bhagavadgita, the non-dual nature of the teaching of Jesus shines out with great clarity. It appears that the message of Christ was an attempt to enable people to recognize once again their own unity with the Divine.

In my experience this is one of the most profound effects of East-West dialogue. It enables us to see afresh the amazing content of the Good News. This in particular is the aim of this book.

Both Vedanta and Buddhism give clear and holistic maps of the development of the human psyche and the way the person relates to God at different levels. Modern Western psychology mainly deals with the human ego and much teaching of religion also stops at this level. Jung has been mainly responsible for introducing the idea of the "true self" into Western psychology—and he studied Eastern teachings. In the maps of Buddhism and Vedanta the self-conscious thinking state is seen to be quite a low-level state.

Often in Christianity, unless one has studied the mystics, there appears to be nothing beyond this level.

It is the need to restore this balance that has sent many Western people to the Eastern religions, although they may not have been able to articulate this need clearly in their minds. Today there is a great need to put Humpty Dumpty together again. People in the Western world have all the material benefits, yet they often feel, isolated, dislocated, and fragmented in their consciousness. It is not the scope of this book to go into the causes of this situation, but it is a state of which we are all aware. The search to reconnect with ourselves and our world and the divine reality is what has spearheaded the search for Eastern wisdom which so characterizes this century. The reflections that are contained in this book are part of this task of reconnecting. Here we are led to a reconnection with our Christian understanding in the light of nonduality.

Reflection

Write down your own personal experience of interfaith dialogue if you have any. This can fall into several categories.

1. Personal experience of other faiths, e.g., visiting their places of worship, visiting friends of other faiths and getting first hand experience of their customs, teaching children in school, attending weddings, funerals, etc.
2. Through your own study or practice, you may have learned yoga, t'ai chi or practiced Buddhist meditation, etc.
3. Through watching television programs on other religions.
4. Reading and study may have brought you into contact with other faiths and their beliefs.
5. Holidays and travel to countries where a different religion predominates.

How much have you reflected on these experiences? Have they affected your own belief system?

How do you see other religions in relation to your own?

How far have you thought through your own beliefs? It could be a very useful exercise to write your own personal creed at this moment in time. Do you see any changes in this over the years?

When you have worked through this book it might be useful to return to this page and see if things have changed.

Chapter 2

Meditation

The primary reason for the level of interest in Buddhism today is its teachings on meditation and its understanding of the human mind. Many people learn meditation in Buddhism or some other tradition because they do not think that such practices exist within the Christian tradition. This is indeed a sad reflection on the way Western Christianity has developed over the past few hundred years. There is a rich contemplative tradition in Christianity, but it is only in the last few decades that people like John Main, OSB, and Thomas Keating, OCSO, have rediscovered and developed this tradition to meet the needs of lay Christians living busy lives in today's world.

Broadly defined, meditation[9] includes those practices that enable people to transcend the rational mind and experience Reality at deeper levels of their being. To touch the deeper levels of being, profound silence is needed. Although outer silence helps, the most important ingredient is inner silence. People in urban, fast moving, media-orientated lifestyles whose upbringing has put great stress on mental activity

---

[9]The word *meditation* in this text is used in the Eastern sense, nearer to contemplation in Western parlance, not meaning reflective prayer as it used to be used in the Christian sense. The Eastern use of the term has taken over in general usage today so we keep to this sense.

and thought processes find inner silence difficult to achieve. Progress on the spiritual path beyond the basic level requires some degree of inner silence.

While contemplation has always been part of the Christian tradition, it is the East that has developed the most detailed and scientific understanding of the higher levels of consciousness in the human person, body, mind, and spirit. It explores the functioning of each aspect of the person and their relationship to each other and the Divine Mystery. In this book I will be using mainly the Buddhist tradition to access this wisdom and show how Christians can benefit from it. It can deepen our understanding of the journey of personal transformation leading to Divine Union. Putting on the mind of Christ,[10] as St. Paul calls it.

The Western science of psychology on the other hand has explored the lower realms of the human psyche, the unconscious and natural drives and needs of the developing human being. The denial of the higher levels and much of the spiritual dimension of the person has contributed to our present day isolation and suffering. The fruit of a negative spirituality that has denied these basic human needs is denial and repression, leading to depression and mental ill health. Repression is a great block to human growth, and thus it is the healing of the split between our spiritual and psychological being which has become the work of the present time. What is happening today is that scholars and practitioners like Ken Wilber[11] are beginning to explore the importance of recog-

[10]Phil. 2:5
[11]See list of further reading for more information.

nising both realms and using them according to the need and level of development of the individual.

The combination of Western psychology with meditation thus becomes a powerful tool for the healing of the whole person. We will work with these tools in such a way as to help restore the contemplative dimension of our lives with a healthy understanding of the human body, mind, and spirit as a unity.

Meditation is essentially a discipline. There are a considerable variety of meditation practices. The purpose of this discipline is to develop a silent mind, open and receptive to the Divine Mystery. In order to achieve this the emotions and their clamoring needs and afflictive dimensions also have to become silent. This is the hardest part of the work of prayer for most people and demands an understanding of the psychological dimension of our being.

People have a tendency to dabble in many things and never take up anything seriously. That is why discipline is needed. It is essential to find a suitable way of meditation and use it over a long period of time, allowing it to transform us. Dabbling is a danger because it is a form of escape. Our wounded egos have to be faced head on. Moving from practice to practice simply comforts the ego and brings superficial peace. What is happening is that the person enjoys the peace of the honeymoon period of a practice and the moment it challenges the ego in any way, it is deemed an unsuitable practice and something new is attempted. Transformation therefore cannot occur until the person settles down to follow a serious spiritual path and stick to it through the suffering and challenges that it is bound to bring.

Meditation with a mantra, a prayer word, is one of the most universal methods and probably the simplest for people leading busy lives. This was the practice that Dom John Main rediscovered within the Christian tradition through his study of the Desert Fathers and John Cassian[12] in particular. *The Cloud of Unknowing,*[13] the medieval English classic, also enshrines this way of practice, which is utterly simple, but not easy because of our complex minds.

John Main was able to rediscover this tradition in Christianity because he had learned to meditate in the East from a Swami in Malaysia, a man who lived and practised according to the aspect of Hinduism known as Vedanta. Vedanta is very *advaitic*, that is, nondual in its approach to God. The True Self of a person and the ultimate ground of being are not two and not one. Swami Satyananda, John Main's teacher was also a disciple of the famous sage of India, Ramana Maharshi, who was a profound advaitin. Ramana Maharshi, often called the silent sage of Arunachala,[14] attracted many Western disciples as well as thousands of Indians. He also had a profound influence on Henri le Saux, Abhishiktananda, one of the first Christians this century to integrate Hinduism and Christianity in his person externally and internally.[15]

Swami Satyananda was clearly also steeped in the eastern understanding of the mantra as a sacred word. *Word* in San-

[12]*John Cassian*, The Classics of Western Spirituality (Paulist Press).
[13]Laurence Freeman, OSB, introduction to *The Cloud of Unknowing*, Element Classics of World Spirituality.
[14]A holy mountain in south India, a place of pilgrimage for Hindus for generations. It became the home of Ramana, and his ashram still attracts pilgrims from around the world although he died in 1951.
[15]See recommended reading for more information on Abhishiktananda.

skrit is *vac,* which refers more to sound and vibration than to meaning. Hence the mantra is a sacred sound syllable whose vibrations have a transforming effect on the person who uses it.

This explains why the Swami was careful to help John Main find a Christian mantra. Using a Christian mantra,[16] the Swami believed, would root and connect him to Christ, not so much through meaning as through sound and vibration. This is clearly reflected in the way John Main referred to using the mantra. Say it, sound it, listen too it. It is also, I believe, reflected in the choice of the word *Maranatha,* which has the long "aa" sound that appears so frequently in Eastern mantras. The number of syllables is also balanced and gives a rhythm that fits easily with the breath. It is also not in the spoken tongue. All Indian mantras are in Sanskrit, which is the ancient language of the scriptures, and is no longer spoken. It is interesting that *Maranatha* is Aramaic, the language Jesus spoke—so once again it connects us to Jesus through sound and language rather than meaning.

In his teaching John Main speaks of the journey of meditation with a mantra being like climbing a mountain and listening to the sound of the mantra in the valley below, growing fainter as we climb, until finally we no longer hear it and enter total silence. This combines the Eastern way of using the mantra with the way John Cassian used it, which was more devotional and closer to the tradition of the Jesus Prayer. When the mantra dies away of its own accord one could say we are then hearing the sound of silence. Also in

---

[16]See Bede Griffiths, "The Way of Meditation with a Mantra," chap. 3 of *The New Creation in Christ* (DLT).

the East sounding the mantra of one's particular or favorite image of God causes one to be united, made one with that aspect of God. John Main uses this idea and shows how meditation causes us to put on "the mind of Christ," as St. Paul called it.[17]

It is clear that these Eastern teachings on mantra illuminated the teaching of Cassian and the Cloud for John Main in a new way. These teachers surely taught this as a way of becoming one with God, but it has not come down to us clearly in the written word. It needed someone who experienced being taught in this way to reopen the teaching for us.[18]

Thomas Keating, OCSO, has travelled a similar path, though his source of Eastern teachings was through transcendental meditation, which has its origins in the same school of Hindu teaching as the swami who taught John Main. While there are slightly different nuances in the way these two teachers offer the work of meditation, they are basically similar.

Another avenue through which meditation is re-entering the life of the Church today is through those who deeply experience Eastern methods and them adapt them to the needs of Christians. Zen is perhaps the most widely used form of meditation in Christianity. Several Christians, most well known of which is the late Hugo M. Enomiya-Lassalle, SJ, have gone deeply into Zen training in Japan and have

[17] 1 Cor. 2:16
[18] Suggested reading: *Christian Meditation: The Gethsemane Talks* by John Main (Medio Media, 1999).

been recognized as roshis. Yamada Roshi, the Master who gave this transmission to Christians, believed that the practice of Zen was sufficiently free of any doctrinal content to be applicable within a different religious framework. As more and more Christians do Zen, this seems to be proving to be the case. Vipassana is another form of Buddhist meditation being widely used by Christians today. Christians are also practicing many branches of Yoga, found both in Hinduism and Buddhism. This helps them to restore a right relationship between body mind and spirit.

How to Meditate Using a Mantra: Sit down, sit upright, still and relaxed. Take a few minutes to become quiet and still. Pay attention to the state of your mind and body at this moment. Breathe naturally with self-acceptance and let go of whatever distraction or concerns preceded the meditation. (Playing gentle music for a few minutes before starting can be helpful.) Then begin to repeat your mantra, or prayer word, gently in your mind and heart. The art is to place your attention lightly on the mantra. Do not fight with the inevitable distractions that come; simply do not give them your attention, keep it on the mantra. Return directly to it when you recognize that you have gone along with any thought pattern, or story line. Keep doing this for the entire time of your meditation. It is helpful to use an external timing device to avoid watching the clock.[19]

---

[19]A cassette with a little soft music at the beginning, blank for the time you wish to meditate, then a few minutes of music at the end is a pleasant way to time your meditation.

Choosing Your Mantra: The mantra that John Main recommended is the Aramaic word *maranatha,*[20] it appears in the New Testament and means "Come Lord" or "the Lord comes." It is helpful to have a mantra that does not have many mental associations that might encourage thought about the meaning instead of attention to the mantra. Other mantras could be: Abba, Father or Jesus or whole or part of the Jesus Prayer of the Orthodox tradition "Lord, Jesus Christ, Son of God, have mercy on me" or a shorter version such as "Jesus, mercy." Words without particular religious connotations such as *love* or *peace*, or *be still*, can also be used. It is important to stay with the same word so that it can become rooted in one's heart. The mantra then is like a little path through the forest that leads us back to our Source and home to ourselves and therefore to God. This practice requires fidelity, perseverance, and trust.

The Journey of Meditation: It is wise to practice meditation on a daily basis, preferably twice daily, morning and evening. The ideal time is half an hour, but it is sometimes necessary to begin with less and over the first weeks or months build up to half an hour morning and evening. It is important that we do not make this requirement another source of guilt or self-blame! If we do not manage the ideal this is not a reason to be negative about ourselves, nor should it be a reason for giving up. Whatever little we do is better than none at all.

When beginning the journey of meditation we soon become aware of the chaotic, distracted state of the mind. In

[20]1 Cor. 16:22 Douay Version.

honestly facing this and going on, the first steps on the journey are taken. This recognition may indicate a need to adjust some aspects of our lifestyle and habits. A typical realization might be the need to watch less television.

It is important never to fight the mind or resist what arises. The thoughts and the turmoil settle down and we begin to move below them until they cease to be a problem. We simply learn to sit and pay attention in whatever way we practice and let all the rise and fall come and go, knowing that nothing either positive or negative lasts very long.

As attention strengthens our focus deepens and becomes more vivid, when this happens deeper levels of the psyche begin to rise. Much of this will be dealt with in the next chapter.

There can also be side effects to meditation, like experiences of heat or cold or shaking or seeing light or color. These are all part of the path and the growth of awareness. Some can be wonderful, some painful, the important thing is not to become sidetracked by them or give them more value or importance than they really have. At such times it is useful to be able to speak to a teacher or someone long experienced in meditation. When we are open and truly seeking God, then whatever we need will be given to us. This is the deeper meaning of the words "give us this day our daily bread." In the East it is said that when the student is ready the teacher will appear. This teacher can come in many guises, and if we have fixed ideas about what a teacher is or what should happen, then we might miss the gift when it comes.

Ways of supporting the meditation practice: The mind and the body need to be nourished and prepared to participate in the journey of meditation.

Some may already have a structure of other forms of prayer and Eucharist to give support. These too may grow and change as the journey progresses and being open to change and new patterns is very important. *Lectio divina* as taught in the monastic tradition is a good way of reading Scripture and other spiritual books as a preparation for contemplation. It suggests taking a short text and reading it slowly a number of times and ruminating on it until its deeper meaning becomes clear to us and we allow it to teach us.

There may also be body tension, stress and stiffness that make it difficult to sit still and erect. Some form of bodywork is often very helpful to the stilling process. Practices such as yoga postures, t'ai chi or chi kung are very useful in preparing the body for the relaxed stillness needed for meditation. All Eastern practices related to the use of the energy in the body including the martial arts and the healing practices like shiatzu and acupuncture can also be useful. The wounds of life are not only stored in the psyche, they are also held in the body and are responsible for much of the stress and distortions that we experience in the physical body. If the body is an obstacle to sitting still it needs to be helped to work through this tension in order to be still. Use of the body in this way can also be a powerful tool in healing the afflictive emotions and patterns of the mind. We are one whole and all aspects of our being need to be involved in the spiritual work.

Art forms such as sumi-e, ikebana, calligraphy, flower arranging, etc., can be very helpful companions to meditation practice. These forms still and focus the mind in the present moment and foster mindfulness.

Spiritual companions on the journey are essential—people

walking the same or a similar path who can support and inspire us. The Buddhist word for this is a *sangha*, a community of practice. This is the reason for the existence of The Christian Meditation Community, which is a worldwide community of meditation groups and individuals. It is vital to be connected to a tradition from which ongoing teaching, instruction and guidance are available. This need not be on a one-to-one basis, but can come through a tradition that offers teaching materials, such as spiritual newsletters, books, tapes and videos supporting the practice.

Nourishing our practice in these and other ways is important if we are to find the strength to be faithful to it. Then one day we will realize that meditation has become central to our lives—we have become committed to the path.

Reflection

I recommend that while reading this book, if you do not already meditate, you give it a try. Follow the instructions in the chapter above and see how it is for you.

If you experience resistance to this suggestion, explore where it is coming from. If your answer is fear, then read the next chapter before proceeding.

If you have doubts about whether this is really prayer, then I suggest you read *Christian Meditation: Your Daily Practice*, by Laurence Freeman, OSB, or any other of his or John Main's books. The one mentioned is the smallest and easiest to read.

Take a little time to look at your relationship to your body and its needs. What could you do about them? The body is very important in prayer and is often the most neglected aspect.

Chapter 3

Meditation and Psychology

S ome think that on the spiritual path it is possible to bypass our own psyche. This is a dangerous misconception. If we believe this we are likely to deny and repress emotional aspects of ourselves when they appear in meditation. The spiritual path is a path to wholeness, and on the journey it is essential that we face and deal with our shadow. We have to face our woundedness and recognize our need for healing at every level of the psyche. The meditations in this book may help in this process of personal integration and transformation of the ego.

People use the word *ego* in various contexts. I use it to mean our personality as it has been shaped, but also wounded, by the circumstances of our childhood and early life. This is our false self, the self that sees *me* as the center of the universe.

The greatest error on the spiritual path is to confuse the ego with the 'true self.' This confusion is present in some Christian spirituality, although the work of C. G. Jung has done much to bring back the concept of the 'true self.' St. Paul speaks of three aspects of the person: body, psyche and spirit. The spirit is the 'true self' and the body and psyche form the personality or ego. When Christianity slips into the body-soul duality, the word *soul* stands for the psyche and the spirit is lost from sight. Our spirit is that part where we are one with the Divine within. The purpose of all meditation practices is to bring us in touch with the spirit. This contact restores the unity and balance of the whole person. When our spirit or 'true self' is in control then the psyche and the body take their rightful place as servants of the spirit. The ego is not something to be destroyed or left behind, as many think. It will be with us until our last breath. Our task is to ensure that the ego becomes the servant of the spirit and that its tendency to repress from consciousness the painful aspects of our nature is healed as far as possible, so that the shadow is owned and integrated into the conscious personality. This is the work of growing in self-knowledge which meditation encourages and enables. It is the ego's efforts to escape this process that often hinders our fidelity to our practice and which encourages the kind of dabbling in spirituality which is so common today.

We have all been inadequately loved simply because of the human condition. No matter how good our parents or others, we suffered moments when we felt unloved, or conditionally loved. This is the essential cause of emotional pain, and it is often compounded by loss, because nothing in this life is permanent. When we face and accept these losses in the process of meditation we grow spiritually and begin to experience the unconditional love of God. Paradoxically, it is only as we experience the unconditional love of God that we can begin to face and heal our wounds. The ultimate cause of our sense of loss and alienation is the loss of awareness of the Divine unconditional love in which all things are held. As St. Augustine said, "The soul [spirit] is restless until it rests in God."[21]

[21]*Confessions of St Augustine* (Penguin Classics).

Some people fear to seek psychological help through counselling or therapy, as they believe this will divert them from the spiritual journey and lead to self-indulgence and unhealthy introspection or even loss of faith. It is clear from the writings of saints and mystics that it is impossible to progress on the spiritual path without facing the shadow. Ignorance of this truth can lead people to give up meditation because they think it is making them unstable. Nowadays there are many therapists trained to include and respect spiritual experience. Meditation and therapy can then work together for the development of the whole person.[22]

When the emotional content rising in meditation is too overwhelming to deal with by paying attention to the mantra, then some counselling support may be needed for a time. On the other hand if no feelings arise over a long time and one feels dry and blocked in meditation this can be an indication that the repressive mechanisms are too strong to release in meditation. This may also be a sign that help is needed. It is important to pay attention to the needs and demands of one's mind and body if growth is to continue.

For many Christians, and indeed others, the issue of self-love and self-worth are of the utmost importance. It is vital to remember that first of all we are made in the image of God. Therefore we must be beautiful and lovable. For one

[22]Therapies with a spiritual dimension include: psychosynthesis, core process psychotherapy and transpersonal therapies. People trained in these should be sympathetic to the spiritual life. Many Jungians too are very spiritual in their approach. It is almost as vital to choose a good therapist as it is a good spiritual teacher. One should not fear to question and explore in this realm while always remembering that we are responsible for our own lives and growth, not the therapist or teacher.

reason or another we were not taught to believe this when we were young. Thus we have grown up with very deep beliefs that we are less than lovable and rarely good enough. These messages and others even more destructive can lie deep within us and control our lives even when we think we have moved beyond them. Thus it is useful to try to discover the basic premises that control our thoughts and begin to change them. They are only thoughts and thoughts can be changed. When we practice meditation, we gain control of the mind and begin to learn that we control the mind and not the mind us. Although this may sound simple it can take many years to really understand and begin to use it, and also to come to know what are the basic thoughts that control our lives. Anger and hatred or resentment, as the Buddha's teaching constantly reminds people, are negative mental patterns that harm us far more than the person(s) against whom they are held. Thus working to heal these mental afflictions is an essential part of spiritual practice. Denial and repression of such feelings and thoughts only makes matters worse. They need to be faced and owned and worked with when they arise until they can be transformed into loving kindness and forgiveness.

This is often a slow work and requires great patience and gentleness with ourselves. Guilt at having these feelings is to be avoided. They are part of the human condition and can only be healed by spiritual practices. This work will be further explored under various Beatitudes.

Reflection

This may be a good moment in which to take a look back over the road travelled thus far on the path of life.

Draw a line or a spiral that represents your life. On this diagram mark both the most significant positive and negative events in your life. Take some time to reflect on the effects of those events. In this way positive and negative can take on new meaning.

Now ask yourself the following questions:

1. What do I think is the most significant moment of spiritual awakening I have experienced thus far? (There may be more than one.)
2. Take time to explore this event and note what effects it has had on your growth to date.
3. What do I see as the most important spiritual practices in my life? How do they affect the way I live?
4. What is my deepest desire at this moment?
5. How do I live with it or try to achieve it?
6. Where do I think I most need to grow?
7. What is the deepest mental statement by which I live? (e.g., I am not good enough.)

When this reflection is completed, keep the notes you have written so that you can return to them when you have been through the whole book.

Chapter 4

The Beatitudes and the Noble Eightfold Path

The eight simple statements of Jesus known as the Beatitudes contain the very essence of his teaching. Most Christians having read them often think they know them well. However their richness can be lost because our minds are loaded with conditioned beliefs and perceptions. We may have been taught to understand them in a particular way that can prevent us from seeing them in other, perhaps deeper, ways.

The transformative power of the Beatitudes lies in the fact that they are written in the present tense and imply realization here and now. They are not promises for the future or for the afterlife! They are states of being that as Christians we are meant to enter into here and now.

The Beatitudes are a course in how to be happy. The meaning behind Jesus' teaching, here translated as "happy" or "blessed," is a profound sense of well being that comes from the transformed self and not the acquisition of wealth or power. I prefer to use the word *blessed* rather than *happy* as it more accurately reflects this sense of rich and unshakeable well being.

In 1994 I was privileged to be present at the John Main Seminar in London. His Holiness the Dalai Lama, who had agreed to comment on passages from the Christian Gospels from a Buddhist perspective, led the seminar.[23] The moment when he read the Beatitudes was one that those present will never forget. The power of that moment lay in the fact that he so embodied what he was reading. There was a sense of having *met* Christ. That a member of another religion could be such an icon of Christ was a profound lesson. Jesus said, "I am the way, the truth and the life." Here we saw one who truly lives the way Jesus lived. He who embodies Christ's teaching and values, becomes truly as Christ was, whether they are members of the institutional religion set up in his name or not. It was clear to all that His Holiness lives in this state of unshakable well being which the Beatitudes call us to. His joy radiates out to all around him in spite of all he suffers from the situation of Tibet and his people. Here is a living example that happiness here and now is a very real possibility.

The Noble Eightfold Path of the Buddha is also a list of means to happiness. In fact it is the Fourth Noble Truth;[24] this is the truth that tells us how to end suffering. This then is the Buddha's list for achieving the cessation of suffering which is the opposite of happiness. The list clearly reflects the teaching that my happiness and that of others are inseparable. What I do to be happy must also make others happy or at least not increase their suffering. We cannot be happy at the expense of others. This is a mistake people often make.

---

[23]The book *The Good Heart* edited by Robert Kiely (Rider, U.K.; Wisdom, U.S.) is the text of this seminar, and is highly recommended to anyone using this book.
[24]See appendix.

Here are the two sets of teachings listed side by side. As we can see they are very different in approach and to some extent in content also. They reflect the basic difference in style we find between Buddhist and Christian scriptures. For a more detailed introduction to the Buddhist teachings turn to the appendix.

THE NOBLE EIGHTFOLD PATH:	THE EIGHT BEATITUDES
BALANCED VIEW; RIGHT SEEING; RIGHT VIEW.	BLESSED ARE THE POOR IN SPIRIT; THEIRS IS THE KINGDOM OF HEAVEN
RIGHT INTENTION, TRUE INTENTION	BLESSED ARE THOSE WHO MOURN; THEY SHALL BE COMFORTED
RIGHT SPEECH	BLESSED ARE THE GENTLE; THEY SHALL INHERIT THE EARTH
RIGHT ACTION	BLESSED ARE THOSE WHO HUNGER AND THIRST FOR WHAT IS RIGHT; THEY SHALL BE SATISFIED.
RIGHT LIVELIHOOD	BLESSED ARE THE MERCI-FUL; THEY SHALL HAVE MERCY SHOWN THEM
RIGHT EFFORT OR ENERGY	BLESSED ARE THE PURE IN HEART; THEY SHALL SEE GOD
RIGHT MINDFULNESS	BLESSED ARE THE PEACE-MAKERS; THEY SHALL BE CALLED CHILDREN OF GOD

RIGHT SAMADHI (a difficult word to translate. It can be rendered as *concentration*, but *contemplation* feels truer to the essential meaning).

BLESSED ARE THOSE WHO ARE PERSECUTED IN THE CAUSE OF RIGHT; THEIRS IS THE KINGDOM OF HEAVEN.

While these cannot be matched one to one, taken as a whole they both cover the essential things necessary for human well being. Right samadhi is the one that least obviously appears in the Beatitudes. It seems to me, however, to be an essential for true purity of heart. This fact perhaps reflects the lack in the Gospels as a whole of any very specific teaching on meditation. We only sense its presence here and there. I am certain that this is because it has been lost, or has come down to us through the oral tradition of the early Church in the teachings of the Desert Fathers and Mothers. Much of this teaching is still alive in the oral traditions of the Orthodox churches.

The term *right* in the Noble Eightfold Path implies an approach that will lead to freedom. It means to be true, on course, being in such a way that will enable us to be happy. One meaning of the Greek word for sin is "to miss the mark." Such an interpretation enables us to see sin as something that destroys happiness, both for oneself and others.

Sin brings its own consequences, rather than the punishment of God. This is something we Christians need to ponder deeply to free ourselves from the fear that the old teaching on sin tended to engender. The fear of hell enhances the fear of death. Fear is the greatest block of all to living in the fullness of life that Jesus came to bring us. It is this fullness of life that is enshrined in the teaching of the Beatitudes.

His Holiness the Dalai Lama points out repeatedly that the one thing all human beings have in common is the desire to be happy and to avoid suffering. Whether a religious person, a business person, a politician, or a criminal, each still has the desire for happiness as a basic motivation; the difference lies in the way one expects to find that happiness.

Some people do not think they deserve to be happy. This feeling reflects itself in a number of ways. Some feel that they are too unworthy and sinful for happiness, that they should be punished and suffer instead. The sad thing is that this can be a deeply held yet unconscious view that prevents happiness from being present. Others feel that it is wrong to be happy when there is so much suffering in the world. Yet if one is not happy it only adds to the suffering of the world! If we are unhappy how can we help and heal others. The power we have to help and serve others will increase according to the level of our own happiness. Thus it is very important to seek to heal any sense we may have that we do not deserve to be happy.

Before turning to the Beatitudes, take a little time to reflect on your attitudes to happiness

Reflection

1. What is your attitude to happiness? Have you ever really thought about this? Why not take some time to do so now?
2. What do you think you most need for your own happiness?
3. Do you believe you have a right to be happy? If not, why not?
4. If you are not familiar with Buddhism I suggest you read the appendix and take some time to reflect on the Buddha's understanding and teaching on suffering and its causes.

Chapter 5

Blessed Are the Poor in Spirit; Theirs Is the Kingdom of Heaven

I n the Gospels, the *kingdom of heaven* and the *kingdom of God* [25] are used interchangeably. Jesus illustrates the terms through parables. He also states that "the kingdom of heaven is within you."[26] (The Hebrew word for *in* and *among* is the same.) In Buddhism the state of enlightenment is spoken of as Nirvana, and the state of unenlightenment as Samsara. At the same time it is said that Nirvana and Sam-

---

[25] Neil Douglas-Klotz, in his book *Prayers of the Cosmos: Meditations on the Aramaic Words of Jesus* (San Francisco: Harper, 1990), explains the meaning of the Aramaic word translated as *kingdom*: "*Malkathakh* refers to a quality of rulership and ruling principles that guide our lives towards unity. It could justifiably be translated as 'queendom' or 'kingdom.' From the ancient roots the word carries an image of a 'fruitful arm' poised to create. It is what says 'I can' within us and is willing, despite all odds, to take a step in a new direction. The word *malkatuh*, based on the same root, was a name for the Great Mother in the Middle East thousands of years before Jesus. The ancients saw in the earth and all around them a divine quality that everywhere takes responsibility and says 'I can.' Later those who expressed this quality were recognised as natural leaders— what we call queens and kings. In a collective sense *malkuthakh* can also refer to the counsel by which anything is ruled, the collective ideals of a nation, or the planet. In this line, we ask that the kingdom/queendom come by clarifying our personal and collective ideas in alignment with the Creator's—toward unity and creativity like the earth's" (20).
[26] Luke 17:21 DV

sara are the same, and that they are both here and now, the difference is in the way we perceive reality.

One of Neil Douglas-Klotz's renderings of this Beatitude is:

> Healed are those who devote themselves to the link of spirit; the design of the universe is rendered through their form.[27]

Douglas-Klotz links this Beatitude with being rooted in the breath as that which links us to the eternal purpose of the universe, the source of life. It is very relevant that in all Buddhist teachings the breath is seen as the best way of being linked to the present moment. Awareness of breathing is the key to being present and therefore seeing Reality as it is.

If the kingdom of God is here and now among us and within us and we do not experience it, this indicates a lack of perception. This lack of perception is usually caused by the fact that we live in the past and its consequences, or in the future and its fantasies. Therefore we tend to miss reality completely because it is distorted by memories and future plans.

Traditionally, we think of heaven as a place, a place that we hope to reach after death, whereas it is a state, a way of being, and a way of seeing. Poverty of spirit is the key to seeing clearly, to shifting our perception so that we experience the Kingdom of Heaven here and now, as Jesus clearly saw it.

What is poverty of spirit? It is what Buddhism calls *de-*

[27]Douglas-Klotz, *Prayers of the Cosmos*, 47.

tachment. This word is often grossly misunderstood and taken to mean indifference, whereas it means non-clinging, non-possessiveness and non-rejection. According to the Buddha life is *Dukkha,* often misleadingly translated as "suffering." There is no English equivalent of *Dukkha*; perhaps the word that portrays it best is "unsatisfactoriness." Life is unsatisfactory basically because nothing lasts, nothing is permanent. Desire and aversion, wanting and not wanting cause the suffering that dukkha creates.

If you pause and look deeply into your life and its present difficulties you will see the truth of this. We suffer and create suffering for others largely because of things we want to have or things want to get rid of. Possessing also implies the desire for permanence in a world where nothing is permanent. "If only I could get rid of this migraine, bad temper, difficult neighbor, etc., I would be happy." "If I could afford to live in the country, find a spouse, be more attractive, popular, etc., I would be happy." Thus the way we see reality is in terms of our desires and aversions. This according to Buddhism is the cause of our unhappiness. It is linked to the fact that even when we do get what we desire, we know it cannot last. Hence even as we enjoy there is always fear lurking, because we know deep within that "this too will pass."

The great illusion is *mistaking the impermanent for the permanent.* This above all applies to the way we see ourselves. The ego desires to be eternal. That is why it is so important to learn to keep the ego in its rightful place. This entails recognizing that it is the spirit that is unborn, undying and uncreated, not the ego. Ultimately, we cling to life and have aversion to death as a result of ego identification. Even though we may not think so, the thing we most cling to is our personal identity, our separateness. Here is the ultimate cause of suffering, the basic cause of our failure to perceive the kingdom, to recognize Reality for what it is. Everything in this world is impermanent, changing, nothing can come with us when we die, not even our treasured ego.

The profoundest teaching in Buddhism is that of emptiness and not-self, *anatta*. This is far from nihilism as many mistakenly think. Rather it teaches that nothing exists in isolation, nothing *can* exist in isolation, everything is interconnected. This interrelatedness of everything is the teaching of *dependent origination*. It also teaches that everything is subject to constant change. Life is a state of flux.

The Buddha's teaching of dependent origination, *Paticcasamuppada,* in Pali is a profound and intellectually intriguing teaching. It is beyond the scope of this book to expound the complex doctrine of the twelve links. It needs only to be seen here in terms of practice, as a device to help us to detach from the idea of a permanent unchanging ego-self, which is a barrier to spiritual growth. P. A. Payutto gives the following comment on its relation to practice:

> The teaching of causal interdependence is the most important of Buddhist principles. . . . The progression of causes and conditions is the reality which applies to all things, from the natural environment, which is external, physical condition, to the events of human society, ethical principles, life events and the happiness and suffering which manifest in our own minds. These systems of causal relations are part of the one natural truth. Human happiness depends on having some knowledge of this causal system and practising correctly within it, through addressing problems on the per-

sonal, social and environmental levels. Given that all things
are interconnected, and all are affecting each other, success
in dealing with the world lies in creating harmony within
it.[28]

All things are linked both in cause and effect and in mutual dependence. You only need to reflect briefly on what
has been involved in bringing your meal to the table to see
the truth of this law. Modern science is proving the truth of
this teaching. Ken Wilber points out in his book *Sex, Ecology
and Spirituality*,[29] that in the world of matter there are no
wholes and no parts. All things are whole-parts or *holons*;
this includes everything from an atom, to a human being,
to the whole universe. Modern science through evolution and
quantum theory shows the truth of this teaching, but does
not apply it to human life and happiness which was the
Buddha's main purpose in teaching it.

If we look deeply into this teaching it helps us to stop
trying to manipulate the universe and the situation of our
lives, and instead to do what Doughlas-Klotz suggests in his
translation of this Beatitude: to live in harmony with the
universe. Some mistake this for quietism, which it certainly
is not. It is summed up best in the Christian prayer: "God,
give us grace to accept with serenity the things that cannot
be changed, courage to change the things which should be
changed, and the wisdom to distinguish the one from the

---

[28]P.A. Payutto, *Dependent Origination, The Buddhist Law of Conditionality*
(Bangkok: Buddha-Dhamma Foundation, 1994). Printed for free distribution.
[29]Ken Wilber, *Sex, Ecology and Spirituality* (Shambala).

other."[30] We can only know the difference and allow change when we have stopped fighting life and trying to force our will upon it. "Father, not as I will, but as thou wilt."[31] This was the prayer of Jesus in Gethsemane. It is often the case that we have to come to our Gethsemani before we learn to say this prayer with understanding.

The Buddha's teaching does not clash with any theological point of view, because he totally refused to engage in metaphysical speculation or debate. He saw this as a distraction from learning how to live here and now. Without going into any theology of the Trinity, it is interesting to note that the idea of the Trinity postulates a relational being at the source of the universe. Is it surprising that God's manifestation should be in the form of interbeing? Thus God and the universe are in harmony, our suffering and unhappiness come about when we lose sight of and fail to accept our place within it.

It is clinging and aversion that create a false sense of an isolated self that is the cause of all our sorrow. In our modern culture, where individualism has become a supreme ideal, we see that this sense of isolated personal identity is causing much misery, mental illness and alienation among people, specially the young. On a global scale it is our failure to see humanity holistically as a part of the planet and the web of life on earth that is bringing us to the brink of self destruction. Not only this, the desire for wealth and power and individual progress is causing ever increasing imbalances between nations that will inevitably lead to conflict and war.

[30]Reinhold Niebuhr's Serenity Prayer.
[31]Matt. 26:39

Yet we still cling to the belief that having what we want leads to happiness, and what this does to others will not affect our happiness.

Poverty of spirit then is simply this: the recognition of our interdependence, above all on God. I know that I have nothing, and can hold on to nothing. I know that Reality is and I am, and the only way to be fully alive is to recognize my "emptiness"[32] and flow with the changing nature of life.

Poverty of spirit is the first and most vital attitude that we need if we want to be happy, contented and fulfilled in this life. *There simply is no other way.* Yet, we all know how much we cling and desire and try to manipulate our environment to suit us. How much we hang on to people, trying to fit them to our needs and calling it love. The simple act of letting go and letting be is not easy. It is something we have to learn and relearn every day of our lives. It is also the first step into the kingdom of Heaven. Unless we begin taking this step, both happiness and the kingdom will forever elude us.

Being caught up in desires and aversions prevents living in the present moment: memories, fears, anger, hatred, jealousy, etc., all the fruits of clinging carry the mind constantly away from the present into the past or the future. Yet the Kingdom of God can be only in the present so it passes us by because even while physically present one is usually mentally and emotionally absent or at best half present. In learning to let go, we become more able to *be* in the present and

---

[32]Sunyata—emptiness—having no inherent isolated existence or 'self' independent of causes and conditions and the parts that constitute the whole.

glimpses of the kingdom begin to appear. Moments of Presence, perfect contentment, oneness with all and unconditional love open up in our lives.

The ego is often confused with the true self. Much modern psychology only deals with ego problems and forming a mature ego. Nowadays many more therapists include the spiritual dimension in their work. The ego is our sense of being an isolated entity, and it is our ego that suffers from desire and aversion and blinds us to Reality. The ego is a tool of the true self and a servant. When in its rightful place, it is useful and necessary, but when it thinks it is the master of the house, then it creates unhappiness. This is not to say the ego must be destroyed; the work of the spiritual life is to keep it in its rightful place and know it. Again the Buddhist teaching of *anatta* or not-self reminds us that there is nothing in us that is permanent, we are forever evolving. The true self is not a fixed identity we can pin down, but is spirit forever moving. This is the teaching that leads to ultimate detachment from self, the hardest detachment of all.

Is detachment not passivity? This is a common difficulty Christians raise in the face of the teaching on nonattachment. The strength of desire makes it impossible for most people to envisage love without attachment. How can there be love without the desire to be loved in return? Even in doing an act of kindness it is difficult not to expect thanks. A world of unconditional love is for the most part beyond our capacity to comprehend. Hence we do not see the kingdom that is already in our midst. The best way to deepen our capacity to perceive this truth of nonattachment is to watch our own little daily unhappinesses and try to trace them back to their source. Invariably, the cause is something we wanted and did not get, or something that came our way that we did not want.

I can hear you say, "This is impossible!" Let us have no illusions, it is hard! If not, we would all be living in the kingdom here and now, and we know we are not. So poverty of spirit is the work of a lifetime, or longer, and it is also the foundation for our spiritual life and the starting point of our journey into the kingdom. There is nowhere to go, nowhere to look, only a way to be. "Be perfect as your heavenly Father is perfect."[33] God is unconditional love and unconditional being, i.e., the source of all beings, capable of innumerable, unlimited manifestations, but also being beyond all name and form, so our life's work is to learn to let go of clinging and aversion. This is what the Beatitudes are about. This was also the main insight of the Buddha's enlightenment and all his detailed teaching is aimed at helping people to see that "the kingdom of heaven is within you,"[34] that Nirvana and Samsara are not different, it is only the way they are perceived and related to. This perception dawns through removing the dust from our eyes and the dark clouds of ignorance from our desiring. Meditation and mindfulness, the Buddha tells us, are the two best tools for this work. Poverty of spirit is the attitude required and may be seen as similar to right view, in the Noble Eightfold Path.

[33]Matt. 5:48
[34]Luke 17:21

Reflection

It is best to take a period of meditation before this reflection.

1. Note your responses and reactions to what you have just read. What "ifs and buts" arise in your mind? Write them down. Read the text several times and watch your mind as it reacts. Seek the reasons for your resistance.
2. Think of a painful incident of the past week, then explore why it was painful and see how it could have been different. Do the same with a pleasant experience.
3. Make a list of your major desires and aversions at this moment.
4. Explore how they affect you. Are they bringing you satisfaction and peace, or discomfort and anxiety?
5. Write down your greatest fears. What effects do these fears have on your behaviour? To what extent do these fears arise from clinging and aversion?
6. Do you remember having an experience of letting go, of poverty of spirit? Write it down and reflect how you felt and what the results were.

Chapter 6

Blessed Are Those Who Mourn; They Shall Be Comforted

"Blessed are those in emotional turmoil; they shall be united inside by love."[35]

Grief is another universal human experience. We all suffer the awful feeling of loss that we call grief. It can come through a death of a loved one, but this is not the only way, there are many levels of loss, e.g., divorce, redundancy, moving house, leaving home, losing wealth, and so on. The terrible grief that comes from losing a child or a parent or a life partner is something that no one in this world escapes. The simple response of Jesus is to point out that we shall be comforted and that grieving is part of the human experience. Jesus also wept at the tomb of his friend Lazarus who had died.[36]

The profound experience of loss creates emotional turmoil with many conflicting feelings that often cause confusion and isolation if they are not understood as part of the natural process of grieving, which in some degree accompanies all experiences of loss. Sogyal Rinpoche in *The Tibetan Book of Living and Dying*[37] has many helpful things to say about

---

[35]Douglas-Klotz, *Prayers of the Cosmos*, 50
[36]John 11:35
[37]Sogyal Rinpoche, *The Tibetan Book of Living and Dying* (Rider, 1992).

grieving and dying. Here he quotes Judy Tatelbaum, who says:

> Grief is a wound that needs attention in order to heal. To work through and complete grief means to face our feelings openly and honestly, to tolerate and accept our feelings for however long it takes for the wound to heal. We fear that once acknowledged grief will bowl us over. The truth is that grief experienced does dissolve. Grief unexpressed is grief that lasts indefinitely.[38]

Comfort in this Beatitude implies that facing grief and working with it, allowing the grief process to unfold with insight, wisdom and awareness allows the grief to be transformed into peace. Very often people who experience a great loss and work with their grief suddenly discover that the person is more a part of them than they were before, but in a totally different way. On the other hand when grief is not faced and lived through, the pain of emptiness and loneliness can linger for years, even a lifetime. Sogyal Rinpoche confirms this when he says:

> Whatever you do, don't shut off your pain; accept your pain and remain vulnerable. However desperate you become, accept your pain as it is, because it is in fact trying to hand you a priceless gift: the chance of discovering, through spiritual practice, what lies behind sorrow. "Grief," Rumi wrote, "can be the garden of compassion." If you keep your

---

[38]Judy Tatelbaum, *The Courage to Grieve: Creative Living, Recovery and Growth through Grief* (New York: Harper & Row, 1980).

heart open through everything, your pain can become your greatest ally in your life's search for love and wisdom.[39]

Not only present grief, but also all our unfinished grieving lies within us, like a lake in the depths of our being. Much of this grief may be from childhood. What would now be considered quite minor griefs can be very big to a child. In the lake of grief in the unconscious they retain the degree of pain they held for the child. Often in meditation one can find oneself weeping for no apparent reason; this is good. Everyone has a river of pent-up tears that have never been shed, and the only way to get them out is to shed them! It makes little difference whether the reason is known mentally or not, the release is just as effective.

Today people are beginning to recognize that one of the results of the denial of death, which contemporary Western society encourages, is that many people are left with grief that has never been allowed to have its say. Instead the grief has been pushed into the unconscious and from there it continues to control our lives. Most of the rituals around death and mourning have gone from our culture. Those in spiritual and psychological circles are becoming aware of the consequences of this denial.

Thus when people begin to meditate seriously they may come up against a deep unnamed sadness. When this is allowed to surface, to be felt and let go, a great sense of release and peace can follow. This experience may return in waves over a period of time. Sometimes help may be needed to explore the sources of the sorrow and make them conscious;

[39]Rinpoche, *The Tibetan Book of Living and Dying*, 316.

at other times it is enough just to experience the sadness and let it go. This is one way of experiencing the truth of this Beatitude.

Another aspect of our society that increases grief is the helplessness that people feel in the presence of death and dying. The capacity to help people to die well or to help them in the hereafter has largely been lost with the decline of religious belief. The sacrament of extreme unction used to be an immediate preparation for death, and was used within the context of a faith-filled preparation for death. Now it has become the sacrament of the sick and is often used more in the context of healing than dying. Some of the reformed traditions of Christianity do not believe in praying for the dead. This leaves an empty blankness around death that increases grief. Yet even for those with no faith in life beyond death, there is a sense in which the dead person's life goes on in those who loved them, and the things they created.

Often at death those left behind experience a sense of guilt or anger because their relationship with the dead person was difficult or unfinished. In these cases practices for helping the dead and working to complete unfinished business can be very important. Funerals when well done can help the process of letting go and saying goodbye.

This subject cannot be concluded without mentioning the work of Elizabeth Kübler-Ross and Dame Cicely Saunders and others who have followed them in the hospice movement, also Dr. Michael Kearney in Ireland and Dr. Balfour Mount in Canada. These are all committed Christians aware of the contemplative dimension of life. There is now much more awareness and consciousness around death and dying, and more people are likely to find the help they need at times of bereavement than was the case less than twenty-five years ago. Buddhism is playing its part in the development of this work. Two striking examples of that are the Zen Hospice in San Francisco and the Rigpa Spiritual Care Programme in London, which has grown up as a result of Sogyal Rinpoche's book on living and dying.[40] You will find suggestions for reading more on this subject in the appendix of this book.

There is a Buddhist story[41] about a woman who came to the Buddha in great distress carrying her dead child in her arms and pleading for his help. The Buddha told her to bring him some mustard seed from a household that had not experienced death and then he would help her. The woman ran from house to house, until she had visited every house in the village, she found no household that had not experienced death. She returned to the Buddha, buried her child and became a nun. She had learned the lesson of impermanence and was able to see the death of her child as part of the impermanence of life. This led her to turn to the spiritual path that could lead her to the Deathless. She was comforted at the profound level of acceptance of death as part of life. When we fully allow death, then we can fully allow life, not before.

Buddhism is sometimes accused of being a life-denying religion because its teaching on this profound truth has not been understood. The deepest mourning can be seen as the suffering of alienation and isolation that human beings feel from the source of unity that contains all things. Buddhism

---

[40] Ibid.
[41] The Pali Canon.

teaches, as Christianity also should if rightly understood, that death is not the opposite of life. It is birth and death that are opposites. *Life* in the true sense transcends both birth and death. When this is realized then true comfort will be found, and it will be possible to let go of clinging to the life of the body and turn to the deathless. That is for Christians the experience of the risen Christ. This is why the goal in Buddhism is to transcend birth and death and so reach fullness of life. Did not Jesus say he had come to give us fullness of life? Surely this is the comfort he promised.

At an even deeper level, Buddhism can lead us to another way of understanding this Beatitude. Buddhism teaches that life is *dukkha*, as we have seen. There is a point on the spiritual journey when everyone with a meditation practice comes face to face with dukkha. This is a sense of separation, an existential sorrow that I exist in separate form. This is possibly what John of the Cross[42] meant by the dark night of the spirit, whereas the grief and pain we have spoken of above can be seen as the night of sense. This teaching on the dark nights can, mistakenly I think, be thought to refer to spiritual states granted only to the special few people called by God to a high state of mystical union. They are in fact part of the spiritual journey of every human being, and when they are not recognized, the suffering they cause may be greatly increased and prolonged.

This is the longing of the soul for God, which nothing in this world can satisfy. It is this longing that leads us into the prayer of union. The longing in our heart grows stronger and stronger the more we meditate and this longing is in

[42]John of the Cross, *The Dark Night of the Soul*, ed. E. Alison Pears.

the end what cleanses all our desires and purifies our hearts. It prepares us for the union with God for which we were all made. The move beyond separate sense into the oneness with all that is that mystics of all traditions speak of in a wide variety of metaphors, poetry etc. Poetry is the best language in which to express the inexpressible.

In existential longing we can only wait for grace and light to dawn. When it does, even through the smallest glimpse of the unity of all in the infinite ocean of Love, then we are truly comforted, we recognize our unity with all that is and we know we are never alone and that we are infinitely loved. If we come to the experience as Christians we experience the risen consciousness of Christ in ourselves and all things. From a Buddhist perspective we recognize our Buddha-nature.

This comfort, which is beyond all other comfort we may receive along the way, is surely the deepest meaning of Jesus' teaching in this Beatitude. If we do not mourn, if we do not freely enter into the experience of darkness and sorrow, then we will never be touched by this liberating awareness. So in very truth we have to go deeply into the mourning and accept it in peaceful surrender in order to move beyond it, to surrender our separateness into the unity of all. This is the deepest level of letting go of ego.

Sogyal Rinpoche's words on grief provide and excellent conclusion to this topic:

> So my heartfelt advice to those in the depths of grief and despair after losing someone they dearly loved is to pray for help and strength and grace. Pray you will survive and discover the richest possible meaning to the new life you now

find yourself in. Be vulnerable and receptive, be courageous, and be patient. Above all, look into your life to find ways of sharing your love with others more deeply now.[43]

[43]Rinpoche, *The Tibetan Book of Living and Dying*, 318.

Reflection 1

Getting in touch with grief and sadness.

1. Find a quiet peaceful place, and lie down in a relaxed position on your back. Focus your attention
   on your breath. Feel as if you are breathing in and
   out of your heart center, the center of your chest.
   (Placing the fingers of one hand on the sternum
   about two inches from the bottom and gently
   pressing may help you to focus on the spot.) Follow
   the breath and watch the sensation in the heart.
   Allow whatever is there to arise. Be with it fully.
   If tears come allow them to flow freely. Just be with
   the sensations and feelings, without allowing the
   memories or stories they bring to mind to interfere.
2. If you keep a journal, or in a notebook, write down
   a list of all the losses of which you are conscious,
   big and small, adult or childish ones. Look at each
   in turn and observe what feelings arise. Allow the
   feelings, but focus on what is now. Avoid becoming
   caught up in the story line of the event, and how
   it could have been prevented, who was to blame or
   whatever. Rather, be with the bare feelings allowing them to rise and to pass.
3. If you contact strong grief with these exercises then
   do them gently, a little at a time. Seek help if you
   need it, if the grief is too much to bear alone. Bereavement counselling helps many people to work
   through the process of grieving until they are able
   to let go. Remember that it is possible to carry
   unfinished grief even from childhood. Many people

hold in their grief for the sake of others, and it needs to be experienced and allowed to pass, if we are to find the true comfort that Jesus speaks of. This is the comfort of acceptance and letting go.

Reflection 2

Praying in Grief and for the Dead. (*Adapted for Christians from* The Tibetan Book of Living and Dying.)[44]

1. Invoke a sense of the presence of Christ. Even if you cannot imagine any form in the mind's eye, just feel the presence strongly and invoke his infinite power, compassion and blessing.
2. Open your heart and call on him with all the pain and suffering you feel. If you feel like crying, let the tears flow freely, and really plead for help. Know that there is someone there for you who embraces you with infinite love and compassion, who knows your suffering. See Christ as your ultimate and nonjudgmental friend. Use the Jesus prayer or any formula of words that comes spontaneously. "Come, Lord Jesus" would be particularly suitable here.
3. Know that Christ responds with all his compassion wisdom and power. Rays of light stream out to you. Sense that light filling your heart up completely, filling you with comfort and bliss.
4. With all the power and confidence this practice brings, imagine you are sending the healing light and blessing of this Presence to your loved one who has died.
5. Send the consciousness of the person you are praying for into the heart of Christ whose presence you are focusing on. In this way allow the person who

[44]Pp. 314–315.

has died to move into eternal light and release any
clinging to that person you may still have.

*Do this practice as often as need be and as in other forms
of meditation do it without expectation of immediate results;
allow the healing to take as long as it needs. This practice of
course does not preclude other Christian forms of praying for
the dead. It can also be adapted to any occasion of suffering,
grief or illness.*

Chapter 7

Blessed Are the Gentle; They Shall Inherit the Earth

The Beatitudes are statements of cause and effect, if you are this or experience that, then the result will be thus. When His Holiness the Dalai Lama spoke on the Beatitudes he saw them as related to the law of karma. The law of karma is that part of the law of cause and effect that operates in the behavior of human beings. Karma is an aspect of the law of dependent origination that is central to the Buddhist understanding of the world. P. A. Payutto defines karma as follows:

> Etymologically, *kamma* (Pali) means "work" or "action." But in the context of Dhamma (Buddha's teaching) we define it more specifically as "action based on intention" or "deeds wilfully done." Actions that are without intention are not considered to be kamma in the Buddha's teaching. Essentially, kamma is intention, which includes will, choice and decision, the mental impetus that leads to action, both creative and destructive, and is therefore the essence of kamma. . . . According to the teachings of the Buddha, all actions and speech, all thoughts no matter how fleeting, and the responses of the mind to sensations received through eye, ear, nose, tongue, body, and mind, without exception, contain elements of intention. Intention is thus the mind's vo-

litional choosing of objects of awareness; it is the factor which leads the mind to turn towards, or be repelled from, various objects of awareness, or to proceed in any particular direction; it is the guide or the governor of how the mind responds to stimuli; it is the force which plans and organises the movements of the mind, and ultimately it is that which determines the states experienced by the mind. One instant of intention is one instant of kamma."[45]

The law of karma, unlike the natural physical laws of cause and effect, involves moral action. In terms of human actions it means that good actions bring good results for ourselves and others, and bad actions bad results. Motivation (intention) therefore is a key factor in determining the karmic results of an action. The above quote shows clearly the degree of personal responsibility that each of us has for the way we are. What we now call conditioning can be seen as part of the complex operation of the law of karma. While we would say that much of our childhood conditioning is not our fault, but something imposed on us by others, the Buddha's teaching indicates that in the long run even beyond the span of this one life we are the creators of our own situation. Whether or not we go along with the law of karma to this extent, we can see how the patterns of our minds as they now are profoundly affect the way we think and act. The essence of the Buddha's teaching is that we, and only we, can work to change the mental patterns we have formed.

[45]P. A. Payutto, *Good, Evil and Beyond: Kamma in the Buddha's Teaching* (Buddha-Dhamma Foundation: Bangkok, 1993). For free distribution.

This enables us to take responsibility for our own actions. Mind training is therefore an essential aspect of growth on the spiritual path, and it is meditation and the mindfulness it helps us to develop that enable us to control our minds and their contents.

Enlightenment takes us beyond the law of karma and outside its operation. Enlightenment can, in theory at least, only be reached when all the fruits of our actions have been experienced. Once we are in a state of enlightenment we do not accrue any karmic results good or bad. This is because we only act from pure altruism in this state, and have no desires or expectations from our actions. This state beyond karma can be seen as total poverty of spirit, the fullness of the first Beatitude, the kingdom of heaven.

The word karma represents a natural law which all experience whatever their religion. The Gospels are full of the concept of karma: "As you sow, so shall you reap,"[46] being the most obvious karmic statement. If we have any doubt about the reality of the law of karma we only need to look around and see how we are all living with the consequences of previous actions and decisions.

If we can recognize here the fact that negative thoughts bring negative actions, then we can see how important it is to change our negative ways of thinking. To replace negative thoughts with positive ones can change the whole direction of our lives. We usually have some deep-seated negative thoughts about ourselves and our lives and these can be the cause of many of the negative experiences we have even

[46]Gal. 6:7

though we may not even be aware of them. If we deeply think and believe we are not lovable, how can love come into our lives?

In the third Beatitude, the consequence of gentleness is inheriting the earth! This is quite surprising because gentleness or meekness has a ring of weakness about it. This passive attitude which we often refer to as a person being a "doormat" has nothing to do with true gentleness.

Gentleness can be seen as the first fruit of poverty of spirit. Look at the life of Christ or the life of Gandhi for instance— they were both men who lived non-violence, *ahimsa.* Here we see two men of great strength. Gentleness is the capacity to act without violence, without in any way harming the rights or the possessions of another person, or ourselves for that matter. Perhaps one reason why it is hard to be gentle with others is because we have not learned to be gentle with ourselves.

One of the fruits of spiritual practice in all traditions is self-knowledge. In order to break patterns of conditioning and turn karmic consequences around, a high degree of self-knowledge and patience is required. To see the patterns of karma in our lives we have to face ourselves with honesty and simplicity. If we bring anger and violence against our negative tendencies they will be reinforced, not healed. Violence breeds violence in us as much as in society.

Some reflection on anger is appropriate at this point. Anger is the great destroyer of gentleness. What is anger? Many people think anger is a sin. It is wrong for a Christian to be angry. It is possible to misinterpret this Beatitude in these terms. Because anger is a strong emotion and can be destructive, it is socially unacceptable, especially for women, who are often conditioned into not admitting anger. It is very important to understand that anger is a feeling, like sadness, grief, joy, or fear. It is simply a feeling, no more, no less. In Buddhism anger is seen as one of the "afflictive emotions," along with greed, hatred and delusion, and is therefore, harmful to our own well-being and growth. This implies that anger afflicts us, and in Buddhism these afflictive emotions are understood to be the main cause of suffering and are for this reason to be overcome. Overcoming is not denial; we cannot overcome anything if we deny that it exists. Owning anger is not the same as expressing anger so as to hurt or harm others; it is then that it becomes wrong. Even wishing harm to others out of anger is already harmful.

The problem with anger is what we do with it in the mind and how we handle it in our lives. Remember that karma is related to intention. We all have anger; we either feel it or we repress it. No one escapes totally from the wounds that produce anger in us. Many people blame themselves and feel guilty for having anger in them. Self-blame leads to self-rejection and this is a form of violence. It also leads to repression and depression. When something is repressed we cannot work with it, but at the same time it controls us from the unconscious. Much of the work of modern psychotherapy is to bring repressed material to consciousness so that we can work with it. In terms of karma, if we deny the patterns of anger in us they will continue to grow in strength and therefore influence our actions more and more forcefully. We will act in anger again and again and thus strengthen the karmic pattern and the negative fruits of anger. Only recognition and self-knowledge make different intention possible. It is impossible to go far on the spiritual journey without facing the shadow and owning the havoc it plays with our lives, especially in relationships.

Jesus told us to love our neighbor *as* we love ourselves.[47] If we are blaming and rejecting ourselves we are not capable of loving others. This is a hard lesson that it takes a long time to learn. If we can bring gentleness to our own anger, we can choose how to deal with it instead of being controlled by it. Even when anger is very powerful and overwhelming, as long as we have some wisdom and insight we can handle it in such a way that it does not prevent us from being gentle. Unconscious anger makes gentleness impossible.

Buddhist insight meditation, Vipassana, can be helpful in working with afflictive emotions. When negative emotions like anger surface from the depths during meditation. The teaching on insight meditation tells us to be aware of what is there, but not to give it our attention. If the anger is allowed, but ignored, it will eventually burn itself out and fade away. Sitting with strong anger and gently keeping our attention on our point of focus, the breath in Vipassana or the mantra in Christian meditation, can be intolerable. When this happens it is important to seek help in dealing with the anger outside meditation. Psychotherapy or counselling may be helpful at such a time. They can be a powerful aid to growth when had in conjunction with a meditation practice.

The result of gentleness according to Jesus is inheriting the earth. That is the last thing we would expect. We would expect that the angry, violent, aggressive person would inherit the earth. Maybe the gentle person will win in heaven,

[47]Mark 12:33

but to say that the gentle inherit the earth is most unexpected. The strength of gentleness is a very real gift, but how does it inherit the earth? Gentleness becomes a reality in combination with poverty of spirit. These two attitudes will lead to a deep contentment and if we are content then in a very real sense we inherit the earth because we enjoy life to the full. We value and enjoy the good things of life without any violence in trying to possess or control them. With grasping and anger gone, this world can reveal itself in all its beauty, and be all ours to enjoy, as it unfolds and passes away before our eyes. The wonder of childhood can return, and the first taste of the kingdom is present. "Unless you become like little children you cannot enter the kingdom of heaven."[48]

It must also be remembered however, that meekness does not equal weakness. True meekness knows how to say "no" when necessary, and also how to express strong feelings when situations call for it. There is a danger of mistaking states of psychological co-dependence or fear, for meekness. Women in particular need to face this issue with deep honesty. People are not being gentle when they allow the weaknesses, faults, or addictions of others to control their lives. They are being codependent and the result will not be gentleness, it will be anger, resentment and disempowerment. Gentleness makes real love possible, and real love can at times be tough, because it will settle only for the real good of the other. There are times when firmness and clarity are essential. Holy people are often hard to live with, because they call us to be true and open to reality.

[48]Mark 10:15

Meekness implies humility. Humility and gentleness go hand in hand. Pride in all its guises tends to make us arrogant and rude. When we feel a need to get our own way or be right then we walk over others. In religious people this can be subtle and disguised and takes the form of passive aggression. The root of the word *humility* is humus, earth. The earth accepts whatever is put on it. The fullness of humility is a very advanced virtue because we cannot pretend to accept while seething inside. This seething creates passive aggressive behaviour, which is destructive of self and others. False humility is both dangerous and harmful. Thus this Beatitude requires a great deal of honesty and patience with ourselves, because as we go deeper in our meditation practice, we will find layers and layers of our ego which react against this teaching.

Douglas-Klotz gives the following rendering of this Beatitude:

> Healthy are those who have softened what is rigid within; they shall receive physical vigour and strength from the universe.[49]

This is a beautiful rendering, which shows clearly the inner state that exists when humility and gentleness are lacking. It is the rigidity of the ego that makes it impossible to be gentle. This inner rigidity can be softened by meditation over time. Mindfulness and a sense of humor bring awareness and lightness to the melting of inner rigidity.

This quote from the Tao Te Ching, which speaks of the

[49]Douglas-Klotz, *Prayers of the Cosmos*, 53.

power and softness of water, beautifully sums up this Beatitude.

> The softness of water
> > erodes the hardness of stone.
> Yielding overcomes unyielding.
> The weak outlast the strong.
> Those who bend
> > endure long after the unbending have broken.
> This is known by many,
> > but practised by few.

Therefore,
> The sage embraces humility,
> > and honours the way of the Tao;
> Lives close to the earth,
> > and welcomes its bitterness.
> So it is that the lowest
> > become the highest;
> And the least
> > become the greatest.[50]

---

[50]Ray Rigg, *The New Lao Tzu: A Contemporary Tao Te Ching* (Tuttle, 1995), 55.

Reflection 1

Take some quiet time to explore your own feelings in relationship to this Beatitude.

1. Do I take full responsibility for my life and actions? Or Do I see myself as controlled by others and the circumstances of my life?
2. How do I see myself?
   An angry person   A gentle person
   A victim   A helper
   A shy person   Defenseless
3. What are my attitudes to anger?
4. Look deeply into your attitude to yourself. Am I able to accept myself, to be gentle with myself? Can I see any signs of repression in myself? What bits of myself do I most reject? What is the basic negative thought or karmic pattern that could be controlling my life and bringing negative results?
5. In what ways do I suffer from guilt? What do I feel guilty about?
6. Do I allow myself to be a doormat, to be walked over by others? Do I stay in unhealthy situations because I am afraid to leave, and call it virtue?[51]

This reflection needs to be ongoing as we move on our spiritual journey deeper and deeper layers of the psyche will surface and things we think were long finished may return again and again and need renewed attention. Patterns reveal themselves

---

[51]If you feel unclear around this question, a good book to study is *Co-dependent No More* by Melody Beattie (Hazelden, 1992).

at deeper and deeper levels so we should not be discouraged when they keep returning again and again. It is also important to have a light touch and let go and move on as soon as possible. This avoids the wrong type of introspection. We look in order to grow, not to be hung up on our shortcomings. Awareness leads to freedom from self-obsession and the true capacity to leave self behind.

Reflection 2

Analytical Meditations for overcoming negative mental states

1. Dealing with Resentment, Anger and Hatred:

Call to mind someone who invokes any of these negative states of mind. Notice how this state of mind feels. Notice how it creates suffering in you. Even though it may never lead to any action, it still causes you suffering and unhappiness. Therefore reflect on the uselessness of having such a state of mind. Then turn your attention to the person in question. Notice how your mind only dwells on and seeks out what is negative about that person. It caricatures them, rather than seeing the whole person. Therefore try to find something good in that person and let the mind dwell on that aspect. This is not to condone what the person may have done, it is what we would say in Christianity: "hate the sin but love the sinner." Then reflect on that person's life. See how they have suffered hurt and harm and how it is this that has created suffering in them. See how they too are seeking happiness and freedom from suffering, just as you are. Then end the reflection by wishing that they may be happy and free from suffering and from the delusions, which cause them to act negatively.[52]

[52]Adapted from B. Allan Wallace, *Boundless Heart*, ed. Zara Houshmand (Snow Lion, 1999).

2. Healing Family Wounds.

Reflect on yourself as a five-year-old child. Reflect on how you suffered at that time within the family context. Feel the pain and misery that you felt as a five-year-old child. See this child's need for comfort and embrace it with loving kindness. Then see your father or mother as a five-year-old child. View their suffering and pain, see the misery of that five-year-old child and embrace it with loving kindness. If need be, go back further and see your grandparent as a five-year-old child and see the suffering of that child and likewise embrace it with loving kindness. Notice how this pattern of suffering, and maybe abuse, repeats itself from generation to generation and have determination to end it here and now, and heal the pattern through loving kindness and healing your own five-year-old child through this practice and other practices in the future. End the practice by sending loving kindness to the family members you have reflected upon and wish that they may be well and free from suffering. This can apply whether the persons concerned are alive or dead.[53]

---

[53]Adapted from teachings and practices given by the Ven. Thich Nhat Hanh.

Chapter 8

Blessed Are Those Who Hunger and Thirst for What Is Right; They Shall Be Satisfied

In the churches today, there is often a healthy stress on issues of social justice, option for the poor, human rights, political freedom, and so on. This Beatitude can validly be interpreted to refer to these issues. The teaching of Jesus is very firm about the need to help others and especially the poor. We are also bombarded by a wide variety of issues and moral dilemmas. Sometimes this bombardment by causes can seem overwhelming and depressing. Through the news media we are brought face to face with so many disaster areas in our world that we often feel helpless and even guilty.

Maybe we are left wondering what right we have to be happy in a world so racked with suffering. Issues of social injustice heighten the awareness that our Western lifestyle is directly contributing to the poverty of other areas of the world. Yet, there appears to be little we can do that will make much difference. This can create a general sense of guilt. Therefore, it is difficult to look deeply at this beatitude. What does it mean to hunger and thirst for what is right?

Douglas-Klotz gives several useful renderings of this Beatitude. He points out that Aramaic words can have many connotations and meanings. Each Beatitude has several nuances, but when translated into Greek they tend to be left with one flavor. Here are several of his renderings to give insights into the implications of "righteousness":

1. Blessed are those who hunger and thirst for physical justice, righteousness; they shall be surrounded by what is needed to sustain their bodies.
2. Aligned with the One are those who wait up at night, weakened and dried out inside by the natural state of the world; they shall receive satisfaction.
3. Integrated, resisting delusion are those who long clearly for a foundation of peace between the warring parts of themselves; they shall find all around them the materials to build it.
4. Healed are those who persistently feel inside: "if only I could find new strength and a clear purpose on which to base my life"; they shall be embraced by birthing power.

These renderings show an inward and outward interpretation, and both are correct and both are necessary. In fact there is the sense that they affect each other and that the inner sense of balance and justice needs to be in place before the world outside can be changed.

Buddhism is founded on the Four Noble Truths of which the cessation of suffering is the third. However in Buddhist countries there can be a lack of interest in the work of development, eradication of poverty, social justice, etc. Buddhists are often accused of being selfish and life-denying, only seeking their own enlightenment and escape from suffering. This comes from their awareness that the outside world cannot be changed until the inside world is transformed. The Venerable Thich Nhat Hanh's[54] life's work has been combining these two aspects through engaged Buddhism. He is not alone in this.

Christianity on the other hand, as the Dalai Lama often points out to his fellow Buddhists, has an excellent track record in service and social welfare. However, Christians can tend to have insufficient awareness of their own inner states. In this case the intention to do good may do harm. Another result of this approach is that attention focused on alleviating the immediate suffering looses sight of the root cause and the long-term effects.

Thus, it is important for Christians to have some understanding of the inner world of justice, guilt, fear, denial, projection, egoism, etc., whereas Buddhists need, as Thich Nhat Hanh and others point out, to be more engaged in the needs of the world. It is clear that this is a matter of balance in which the two religions can help each other. This balance is represented in both religions by the two pillars of wisdom and compassion. For a sound building, both pillars need to be strong.

There is a negative redemption theology that can produce an attitude to the suffering of Jesus that leads to psychological guilt and fear. In my experience people who have been taught as children that their sins crucified Jesus carry this deep in their unconscious. Such teaching affects children

---

[54]Vietnamese Zen Master, author of *The Miracle of Mindfulness*, *Being Peace*, and many very readable books about living, which reflect the attitudes of the Beatitudes. He now lives with his community in Plum Village in the south of France. He is famous for his work for peace and especially in the West for helping veterans of the Vietnam War.

deeply as they do not have the intellectual understanding needed. Buddhism can help us to clarify our thinking and our attitude to suffering. Seeing it as the ripening of the fruits of our own actions and attitudes can be a healthy counterbalance to the above.

God participates in humanity out of unconditional love. This love threatens the structures of power people build up. Jesus lived in total Love and Truth and people were afraid; this fear led to his death. It is so easy to seek to destroy what we fear. Because Love is eternal, the death of Jesus broke the bonds of death and showed us the way to eternal life. His total self-surrender through death to new life in the resurrection needs to call forth love, joy, and gratitude, not guilt and self-hatred. The Orthodox churches have stayed truer to the meaning of the resurrection. They see God as becoming man in order that man might become God. This is far from the negative, sin and hell teachings of some Western Christian denominations, particularly in the last couple of centuries. While much of this has changed today, it lingers in the views of many that no longer go to church. This in my view is a main factor in the numbers of people turning to Buddhism today.

Basically, there are two types of suffering; one is natural, it belongs to being in this world. That is the suffering around old age, sickness, and death. This is the lot of all living beings, animals and humans. The other suffering is that which human beings create for themselves in the face of the reality of old age, sickness, death, and impermanence. This is the suffering the Buddhists call *dukkha*. The Buddha teaches that this type of suffering is unnecessary and is removed by letting go of clinging and aversion. If we can transcend self-created suffering, then the pain of old age, sickness and death will lose their power over us. Such an understanding can change our approach to this Beatitude and to life.

Where in this scheme of things does the suffering which human beings inflict on each other find a place? Clearly, it is part of the karmic consequences of the actions of the human race as a whole. In Christianity, too, we talk of corporate or collective sin. Whatever our beliefs about life after death, this will always remain a mystery.

In our vocabulary the word *right* implies that there is its opposite, *wrong*. The word *wrong* has a moral tone to it. One of the teachings in Buddhism concerns the reconciliation of opposites. Both poles are needed to make the whole. Things only become negative and harmful when they are split from wholeness. This may seem a strange concept at first. Take the human person for instance, that part of the self which is not in consciousness, that is pushed away, denied and split off, is the part that causes us to be negative. When things are allowed back into consciousness and are recognized as part of us they cease to be harmful unless we then choose to act harmfully. Then we can see right as being the way things naturally are. When God had finished creating the world, the Book of Genesis tells us that he saw that it was very good[55] (old age, sickness, and death were part of what he saw!). The way of things or the Tao, as the Chinese call it, is the flow of life as part of an infinite whole. Opposites are

[55]Gen. 1:31

the creations of the human, judging mind. These categories come from our experience of pleasure and pain. Much moral law has evolved from this experience of opposites.

This is an important point, but one which is not easy to grasp. We are dealing here with different levels of truth and reality, ultimate truth and relative truth. Both are true and real in their own way. One level of reality does not negate the other, as people sometimes mistakenly think. We need to integrate the world of duality into the world of nonduality. Most people deny the nondual level and think that duality is the only reality. This is vitally important in relating to good and evil. In the realm of nonduality all is part of God. This must include the shadow, that which we call evil. If it does not, then God is not God. When a person has grasped this they are able to stop projecting their own shadow onto God, the devil or other races, etc. A glimpse of nonduality, I believe, is essential for the healing of our splits and projections. Without it we remain in illusion and our god remains a projection of our human psyche.

From this perspective it is clear that the ills of the world come from the split consciousness of humankind and their rejection of one level of Reality. Therefore the way to hunger and thirst for what is right is above all to heal the split in ourselves, so that we can be of real service to others.

When we reflect on this Beatitude we need to be aware of our own views and opinions of what is right. These cause judgments that may be misguided. It is wrong views that cause work done for good causes, with supposed good intentions, to do more harm than good. Here again we face the importance of awareness of our own motivation.

One of the skillful means in the Noble Eightfold Path is

"right livelihood." Doing work that enhances Reality, living in tune with the flow, not doing things that increase the divisions and the destruction which have come about through the divided psyche of humanity. Work that does not harm others the environment or ourselves. Work will then be part of a healing and growth process for ourselves and others. This frees us from the need to manage, control and fix ourselves and our environment. As Lao Tzu paradoxically states: "The sage does without doing, works without effort, teaches without words."[56]

The outcome of this Beatitude is satisfaction. We will be content with the way things are and all our actions will be in tune with Reality. When we are truly content and at one with life and ourselves then we will find the resources to make our best contribution to the disaster areas. If we see it in terms of healing the splits in life rather than putting right what is wrong, then our approach will be healing.

It can be useful to look deeply at the causes we support, the charitable works that we do, and the choices and reasons behind the things we undertake in the external world. Why is it that we espouse this cause rather than that? Maybe we choose a cause or a particular issue of justice to meet a need that is in us. For instance someone who wanted children and could not have them may be deeply involved in children's charities. Someone who had an abortion when they were young and suffered guilt from it, may go out and become a campaigner in a pro-life organization. Or somebody who has experienced a particular disease may work for those who suffer from this

[56]Rigg, *The New Lao Tzu*, 11.

disease. This can be a positive way of meeting our needs. The contribution we make will be more useful if we are fully aware of our motivation. This is the way we are satisfying a particular hunger or thirst that we have.

Awareness of this type enables us to recognize that our actions are not totally altruistic and will help us avoid the danger of using other people's suffering to meet our own needs, which creates an attitude of self-righteousness. Such a conscious approach can also help avoid burnout. If we are unconsciously striving to meet a personal need through "helping" others, our level of emotional involvement will probably harm us and the people we are trying to help. This invariably leads to burnout or breakdown.

It is also important to remember that we cannot actually change anything, least of all another person. We can only create the conditions conducive to change. If we are trying to change others, failure leads to guilt and we find ourselves carrying an intolerable burden that is harmful to us and to those we hope to change. Burnout is the result. This is perhaps why it is so prevalent in the helping professions. Doctors and health care practitioners are particularly vulnerable. If they forget that every one must die in the end and come to see death as a failure of their work, then they will suffer great stress and anxiety. Often we know these things in our heads, but are unaware that our emotions are responding differently. This is why personal spiritual practice is so important if we are to be of real service to others.

The peace and satisfaction of which Christ speaks in this Beatitude will only be ours when we have at least begun to understand the importance of selfless service. Doing all we can, but expecting *nothing* in return. This is an aspect of letting go that is very hard to learn. We all want something from the work we do, yet, until we can learn to work without seeking reward, true satisfaction will always evade us. In Buddhist teaching the way to break the cycle of birth and death is to cease to create karma (consequences), and the only way to do this is to act purely, without trying to dictate or control or gain anything from the outcome.

Reflection

1. After a period of meditation or quiet reflection write a list of all the causes or charities you are involved in or support financially.

2. Linger on each in turn; observe your reactions and feelings in each case. Note any feelings of guilt, sadness, or anger etc. that may arise, explore these to see where they come from. It may take time to do this. Do not be afraid to return over and over again to areas of uncertainty, observing your reactions.

3. Make a list of all your goals in your work and in your life as a whole. Reflect on your emotional reactions to reading these slowly one at a time.

4. Can I see my work, hobbies etc. as "right livelihood?" If the answer is no to any of this, relax and explore the situation thoroughly. Spend time with the fourth rendering of this Beatitude. Allow it to speak to your heart in silence. Knowing that change comes when we open to new possibilities, let go of feelings or pressure or guilt, allow a new way of being to come to birth in its own time.

Observing without judgment is very important in such exercises. Allow yourself just to look and recognize, "Ah! That's how it is." The first step to healing is seeing without judgment; the rest tends to follow in its own time! This is the meaning of "The sage does without doing."[57]

[57]Ibid.

Chapter 9

Blessed Are the Merciful; They Shall Have Mercy Shown Them

The two energies of divinity most stressed in Buddhism are Wisdom and Compassion. In Mahayana Buddhism they are personified as the two great Bodhisattvas, Avalokiteshvara (Chenresig in Tibet) and Manjushri. Mercy/compassion/love are central qualities to be developed in all major religions. Jesus said, "Love your enemies: do good to them that hate you."[58]

What we often fail to realize is that from a purely psychological perspective this teaching is impossible. Compassion and mercy are not qualities that arise naturally when we are hurt, persecuted, abused or injured; rather our natural responses tend to be anger and revenge. The eye for an eye and tooth for a tooth mentality is the only language the ego knows. Christians sometimes suffer greatly because they know Christ teaches forgiveness and mercy, but they find they cannot *feel* forgiveness or mercy and the result is guilt, in addition to the other sufferings which have caused their angry or vengeful feelings in the first place. Recognizing that feelings alone are neutral, that the reality of forgiveness and mercy lie beyond feeling, can be a liberation in itself.

What the Buddhist teachings on mercy and compassion

[58]Matt. 5:44 DV

show us is that the ego is incapable of producing mercy of itself. Mercy, compassion and forgiveness have to be developed through spiritual practices that draw on energy beyond the ego. This is the realm of spirit. Equally their opposites have to be fully owned and recognized in ourselves before we can be free from them. Compassion and mercy flow when we open our hearts to the Source, Being, God, Christ, Buddha nature, depending on our belief system. "Without me you can do nothing!"[59]

Meditation itself, if practised honestly and regularly, brings us face to face with our negative emotions, our envy, anger, revenge, etc. and then opens to us the Source of Wisdom and Compassion. This is a subtle process. When we meditate, the negative feelings we normally repress are released into consciousness. It is very important that this happens. It is a sign of growth, not the opposite as we often think. As long as these emotions remain repressed and unconscious they cannot be healed and we will remain incapable of compassion. When they do rise into consciousness, it is extremely difficult not to allow our attention to get absorbed in the thoughts, memories, and story lines they generate. Thus it is at moments like this that the greatest discipline is needed to return to our point of focus, our mantra. If these feelings are intolerable and we cannot do this, then we need to seek help in the form of good counselling or therapy. This is a very delicate and important point as much time can be wasted in indulging these feelings in meditation and if we do this we run the risk of strengthening them instead of letting them go.

[59]John 15:5

That is the negative side of developing mercy. The positive side consists in learning to practice in a way that fosters mercy and compassion in ourselves. The Buddhists have many ways for doing this; I will mention a few briefly. The first basic step is to reflect on the possible reasons behind the actions of those we hate or cannot forgive. Reflect on their sufferings or what these might have been if we do not know. Reflect on our negative feelings and how painful they are, while doing so recognize that these feelings and the pain they generate are universal. My suffering, my anger, my hate are the same suffering, anger and hate that others experience, that my enemy feels. They are not my anger, hate, etc., they are just anger and hate, they are part of the universal cause of suffering. Reflections such as these can bring us to a more balanced view of things through the use of the rational mind.

However, the rational mind is very limited in its scope. To really develop mercy, forgiveness and compassion within ourselves we need to identify with Divine Mercy. As Christians this comes to us in Christ. Thus a good practice taken from Tibetan Buddhism is the Tonglen[60] practice which involves a process of exchange and can be done with the help of the imagination. Become conscious of the indwelling presence of Christ, through you Christ takes in the pain and suffering of the other and sends mercy and compassion in its place. This can be done with our breath. Breathe in the suffering, pain, etc., of the enemy or other loved one who suffers, and breathe out through yourself the love of Christ, the forgiveness of Christ, etc., towards the other person, the enemy or suffering loved one. In Buddhism the primary pur-

[60]Rinpoche, *The Tibetan Book of Living and Dying*, 193–95.

pose of this practice is to develop mercy and compassion in oneself, if the other is helped this is seen as a side effect. It is useful as Christians to reflect on this. We are often so busy doing good to others that we fail to take adequate notice of ourselves. Buddhism always reminds us that it is only ourselves that we can change and in changing ourselves others are also freed to change.

This is a good point at which to touch on the question of petitionary prayer. This is practiced widely in Christianity. What do we mean and what do we believe we are doing when we promise to pray for something or someone in need? Often prayers of petition sound as if what we are doing is telling God something we think he does not already know. Or we are asking him to change his mind about something. Put like this, it is easy to see that this is absurd. There can be nothing God does not know, and we cannot know better than God. So what are we doing?

Many people who have been meditating for some time begin to have difficulty with petitionary prayer. This is usually because their understanding of God is beginning to change. The benevolent (or not so benevolent) parent image of God, which most of us have buried deep in our psyche from childhood, shifts. God becomes more mysterious, but more present and real at the same time. Thus our understanding and use of petitionary prayer changes also. It is often a way of reminding ourselves of the needs of the world. It is probably most often a way of trying to help when we feel helpless in all other respects.

The Tonglen practice mentioned briefly above can be a way of bringing petitionary prayer to new life. We know that all things are interdependent and connected. Modern science, as well as Buddhism, tells us this, not to mention St. Paul in his images of the mystical body of Christ. A practice like Tonglen can enable us to realize that we are called to actually participate in the work of compassion and healing which is Christ's work of redemption. St. Paul speaks of "making up in my flesh . . . what is lacking in Christ's afflictions for the sake of his body, that is, the church."[61] The Bodhisattva ideal in Mahayana Buddhism can enhance our understanding of this teaching.

In taking the Bodhisattva vow, one who is seriously on the spiritual path makes a vow not to go to Nirvana, full liberation, until all sentient beings are saved, liberated. In this vow they commit themselves to stay within reach of suffering in some way or other in order to alleviate it, until all is complete. Thus Buddhists see Christ as a great Bodhisattva. This idea can also give us a fresh view of redemption, and enable us to see how we play our part in it. This type of practice can also be very helpful in situations where we may be with a dying person who can no longer connect verbally. Silently entering into the pain of another in this way is powerful and healing. The prayer of silent participation can help to remove the helplessness as to how to pray in a particular situation. Above all this is a powerful way of opening the heart in compassion.

Mercy in its turn comes to us in its own time and way, the gentle touches of the unconditional love of God in Christ, can reach us the more we reach out to others. This is the heart teaching of this Beatitude. The opening of the eye of the heart is an ongoing spiritual process, which a

[61]Col 1:24 Revised Standard Version

deepening understanding of all the Beatitudes will surely enable in us. His Holiness the Dalai Lama has pointed out many times that the more we try to serve others and make others happy the happier we ourselves will be. This comes from the Bodhisattva ideal, which includes the wish not to go to Nirvana until all sentient beings are saved.

> Whatever joy there is in this world
> All comes from desiring others to be happy,
> And whatever suffering there is in this world
> All comes from desiring myself to be happy.[62]

This idea is also reflected in many Buddhist prayers, like this one which is said by all Rigpa students after their practice:

> By the power and the truth
>   Of this practice,
> May all beings have happiness
>   and the causes of happiness
> May all be free from sorrow
>   and the causes of sorrow.
> May all never be separated
>   from the sacred happiness
>   which is sorrowless
> And may all live in equanimity
>   without too much attachment
>   and too much aversion.
> And live believing in the equality
>   of all that lives[63]

[62]Bodhisattvacharyavatara VIII:129
[63]Rigpa Buddhist Centre, source unknown.

Reflection

A Compassion Meditation on the Heart of Christ Adapted from Tonglen as explained in the Tibetan Book of Living and Dying.

(A suitable setting can help to create the right atmosphere. This practice can usefully be done after an ordinary meditation period when the mind is more calm and focused. It may be helpful to read the following instructions slowly on to a tape allowing pauses of whatever length you wish where ellipses occur in the text and then going through the prayer with the help of the instructions.)

Sit still and upright, breathing normally. Focus your attention on your heart center, which lies in the center of your chest between your breasts, not on the position of your physical heart. Begin to imagine you are breathing in and out of this heart center, rather than through your nose or mouth. . . .

Notice how your heart center feels. Sometimes it feels like a stone, or as if it has an iron shield in front, at other times it may feel warm and open. . . .

Become aware that here at the deepest center of your being you are one with the Heart of Christ, the Compassionate Source of the universe. His love flows on your breath as you breathe in and out. . . .

You can visualize this love as light or sense it as warmth or whatever is helpful for you. Allow it to pour freely through you. . . .

Focus your attention on any part of yourself which you do not like or which you reject. Let all your dark corners be brought into focus. As you breathe in draw all your dark and unloved parts into the heart of Christ, as you breathe out let his love flow to every corner of your being. . . . Do this for as long as you need. If there is something you cannot face, do not force it. Know that in time all will come into the focus of Christ's love. . . .

Return to breathing through the heart center for some moments. . . .

Now call to mind your family, those you most love either by naming or visualizing them; as you breathe in, draw all their darkness and pain into the heart of Christ and breathe out Christ's Compassion to them. . . . Do this for as long as is helpful. . . .

Let them go and return to breathing in and out of the heart.

(Repeat this with other categories, e.g., those who have asked for your prayer, a particular sick person, a troubled area of the world, all suffering, the planet. If it helps, suffering can be seen as black smoke and breathed into Christ's heart that way. If you find this in any way threatening or frightening, do not force yourself; only do what you feel comfortable with.)

Finally call to mind the most difficult relationship in your life. Bring that person before you. Begin by breathing out good wishes to them, may they be well and free from harm. . . . Know that the unconditional love of Christ has already forgiven all; see if you can breathe in the pain of the situation to Christ's heart and breathe out his love and forgiveness; know it is not your forgiveness but universal forgiveness in which you can participate when you are ready. . . .

Bid that person farewell and return to breathing in and out of your heart. When you are ready end your prayer in any way you find helpful.

(You may need to work with this last part many times before it feels really resolved and compassion and forgiveness can flow. It can be a powerful tool for healing wounds even if the person concerned has died; healing and forgiveness transcend death.)

Chapter 10

Blessed Are the Pure in Heart;
They Shall See God

This Beatitude leaps out from among the rest as the most amazing. In the Old Testament we read that a person cannot see God and live.[64] Here we are told that the pure in heart see God. Our response may be to think that purity of heart is impossible for us, or else we assume that seeing God is something reserved for another life beyond. This conditioned thinking prevents us believing and really accepting what Jesus says. It is important to see the true depth of meaning and the implications in this Beatitude for here and now.

"Purity" is a word the Christian has to think clearly about; it is a word loaded with conditioning from the past. Purity often seems to imply a kind of sexual innocence that in fact has little or nothing to do with Jesus' use of the word. Every religion develops taboos and ideas of ritual purity, freedom from sin or contamination of any kind. Ultimately purity of heart includes purity on all levels of our being. But purity does not imply virginity or a denial of sexual pleasure and fulfillment, but rather the full, right, and balanced use of all aspects of relationship. Confusion about this can prevent

[64]Exodus 33:20

people from aspiring to purity of heart and prevent them from fully grasping the meaning of these words of Jesus.

We can never make ourselves pure. No amount of abstention or keeping of rules will bring us to the purity of heart of which Jesus is speaking. Often ritual purity and spiritual pride are discovered to be bedfellows. If we think we are pure, then the chances are that we are proud. It was this false purity on which the destructive teaching of Jansenism was formed. It was said of the nuns of Port-Royale, that they were as pure as angels and as proud as devils.[65] Much of the extolling of the virtue of virginity and chastity has grown from this false view of purity.

What then is true purity? In the Sanskrit scriptures of Hinduism and Buddhism two words are found which will help us with this. One is *ekargrata* and the other *viveka*. *Ekargrata* is best translated as "one-pointed." It implies a seeking of truth above all else: the kind of drive towards Truth, Wisdom, and Love that sports people have towards the trophy or world title. Everything else stands second to the first goal of life—"seeking God." This is the one quality that St. Benedict sought in those wishing to enter his monasteries. When we remember that God is in everything this need not be seen as negative renunciation, but living life— pure, naked life—to the full, for which we were born. *Viveka*, on the other hand, means the ability to distinguish between the transient and the eternal. This enables one to recognize the truth when it appears. These two elements give the capacity to develop the purity of heart that Jesus speaks of here. Meditation combined with awareness in the present

---

[65] A Parisian convent that was a center of the heresy of Jansenism.

moment, or mindfulness, are the essential means to develop these two qualities, nothing else can really achieve this combination of attitudes.

Looking back on these reflections, it seems clear that purity of heart is the fruit of beginning to live the previous attitudes. First of all purity of heart requires poverty of spirit. As long as there is clinging to things, events or people, or even to ideas of God, it is not possible to develop the one pointed vision which purity of heart requires. Meekness, gentleness, or humility is another essential, for as long as there are any lingering ambitions, especially spiritual ambitions, there is no seeking truth as it is, but only for what it can deliver. The type of mourning which leads to facing a sense of separateness and isolation requires a capacity for solitude, which is not the same as loneliness or being alone. Solitude is the capacity to rest in the 'self' (spirit) and know that there is within, all that is needed for the process of transformation. Solitude teaches that no one else can do it for us. The steps towards purity of heart can only be taken by ourselves in the here and now.

Hungering and thirsting after truth in every aspect of life is another attitude that is necessary for the vision of Reality, which is God. Mercy too is essential, for as St. John asks, "How can we love God who we do not see if we cannot love the brother or sister we can see?"[66] In other words if we cannot see God in others, then we will never be able to see him in himself. Before we can see him in others we have to see him in ourselves. When all these attitudes are beginning to take root in a person, even to the smallest extent, then it

[66] 1 John 4:19–21

becomes possible to have fleeting glimpses of Reality, or life as it is, of the unconditional love in which the universe is held. "In him [God] we live and move and have our being."[67]

This is why people turn to meditation, because it is the most direct way to purify our vision sufficiently so that we begin to be able to see God in ourselves, in others, and in all that is. It is what the Fathers and Mothers of the desert call "pure prayer." This is something that one cannot explain to anyone who has never glimpsed it, even as one cannot describe color to a blind person. When we become able to "see" without the filter of the mind, only then does this Reality slowly dawn. As we meditate we listen deeply to the word in ourselves. As our attention to the mantra grows finer and finer we are able to look deeply into ourselves, not look at ourselves, or think about ourselves. To look deeply to the source of our being is silence, until the dawn comes, and we "see" who we are and our place within the unity of things. Then we are in God.

[67]Acts 17:28 RSV

Reflection

Meditation is an important means for the work of moving towards purity of heart. Two periods of meditation daily are strongly recommended. It is helpful to have a particular place in which to practice. This creates the awareness and intention in oneself for approaching this work of silence, stillness, and simplicity. Here briefly outlined is the way of Meditation as redeveloped by John Main, OSB.

Choose your place and time carefully. Spend a few moments preparing for your meditation. Some simple yoga stretches or t'ai chi or chi kung can be most useful, or listening to relaxing music; even having a mindful shower and change of clothes can help set the tone. Having an icon, and/or flowers, candle, incense, etc. can all be helps to creating the right attitude of mind for practice. Reading of Scripture or the Divine Office can also be helpful, though this might be more fruitful after meditation, when the mind is calm and receptive for the words of Scripture.

Sit down and sit still. The only rule of posture is to keep your back straight; this promotes deep relaxation and allows your energy systems to flow freely. The spine should be allowed to take its natural upright position, the chin pointing towards the chest to avoid neck tension.

Check your body for tension, and relax those parts where you carry tension e.g. shoulders, neck, jaw. Become aware of your breathing and allow it to flow naturally. Lightly close your eyes and gently begin to repeat your mantra or prayer word. This can be any scripture word or phrase meaningful to you, e.g., Abba, Jesus, the Jesus Prayer, or the word that Fr. John Main recommended which is *maranatha*, said as four equally stressed syllables, with a long "a" sound. MAA—RAA—NAA—THAA. Once you have chosen a word, always use the same word; then it becomes rooted in your heart and stays with you at all times.

Gently repeat the mantra for the whole time of your meditation. Pay attention to it lightly, do not use it as a weapon against your thoughts and feelings, but as a simple point of attention to which you return every time you realize you have stopped paying attention to it. As you say the mantra, listen to it and allow it to move from the head to the heart.

Do not repress or deny thoughts or feelings, especially feelings. Acknowledge them, but return your attention gently to the mantra. This way, followed with simplicity, fidelity, and openness will lead you to silence. In this silence purity of heart is born. We learn to meditate without any expectations or demands.

As our meditation develops we learn slowly how to let go of all expectations or demands in our practice. As we let go the mind becomes more and more relaxed and open, the mantra very soft and gentle, sometimes almost inaudible. The mind needs to stay alert and vivid, not to lose awareness or sink into a cloudy sleepy state. If this happens stronger attention to the mantra is needed. Then almost as it were between breaths, we get glimpses of . . . "the sky-like nature of Mind" as Sogyal Rinpoche calls it . . . The ground of being . . . nonduality . . . at this point words fail.

Chapter 11

Blessed Are the Peacemakers; They Shall Be Called Children of God

Just as the first five Beatitudes lead to purity of heart and contain the elements needed to become pure in heart, so these last two are the fruits of purity of heart. Peace is much sought after today and yet is so hard to find. True peacemakers are rare because no one can truly bring peace to a situation if they do not have it themselves. Although we long for happiness, we know we cannot be truly happy as long as peace of heart eludes us. The Beatitudes that come before this point to peace. If they are lived then peace of heart will appear and peacemaking will happen naturally. In the words of Thich Nhat Hanh men and women are called to "be peace!"

What is peace? What is Jesus telling us to be makers of? His peace is not merely absence of war, nor even absence of conflict, not peace at any price. Basically, I think the peace of which Jesus speaks is a calm tranquil state of mind in which the individual is no longer torn here and there by unfulfilled desires, unfinished business, bitterness, anger, or delusion, which includes clinging to views and opinions. Above all it seems to require the absence of greed and envy. Greed in Buddhism is seen as one of the basic enemies to spiritual growth. The simplest definition of greed is wanting more than we need, and envy is wanting what others have. Greed and envy are the root causes of war and conflict.

Often people on the spiritual path feel that greed and envy are not things they need to worry about. But in fact there are many subtle ways of being greedy that are almost endemic among spiritual seekers. Wanting spiritual experiences is a subtle form of greed that most meditators have to deal with. Greed can also creep into our way of seeking. Looking for more and better practices that will give us more fulfillment, more insights, more spiritual experiences, will make us look and feel good. Greed for fulfillment is perhaps one of the greatest enemies to true spiritual practice in our modern world. It often keeps people restless, and unpeaceful, because they are always looking for something better than they have. This not only leads to restlessness and unrootedness, it also leads to conflict and competition in spiritual matters, which destroys community. Envy too of course is equally destructive. The desire for what others have in terms of positions or relationships has broken up many a community and led to thoughts, words and deeds completely contradictory to peace. This type of envy often manifests around spiritual teachers, each disciple wanting to be the favorite, or at least to receive special favors. It was present among the disciples of Jesus. On one occasion James and John[68] asked Jesus if they could sit on either side of him in the kingdom, and the others were indignant. His answer was to ask if they could be true to him through all that would happen. They said they could, but in the event all failed. This is a very salutary lesson for everyone. Jesus also

[68]Mark 10:35–41

said that the last would be first in his kingdom![69] Who of us is really willing to be the last?

Peacemakers are those who are able to see and appreciate the good in other people, other countries, other religious systems. Not only see it, but recognize and praise it and learn from it without trying to conquer it, take it over or use it to enhance themselves. This is something that needs to be looked at closely when we engage in inter-religious dialogue. In the past, Christianity has been the religion of the empire building, conquering and 'culturally superior' Western powers. These qualities not only destroy peace, they are in danger of destroying the planet. Christians have to be careful to approach others with respect and reverence and not enter dialogue with the unconscious motive either to convert or to plunder others' riches to use for the gain of their own church or teaching. This of course does not exclude peaceful and respectful sharing of gifts. Any more than peace between nations should prevent trade or cultural exchange. Trade should never be plunder and exchange, never rape. The West has been and still is guilty of both on a large scale. Christian institutions played their role in this too.

The churches have undergone a major shift in this regard as have many missionary institutes, especially within the Roman Catholic Church. There have been deep changes of heart that have led to heroic work being done by Christians in the cause of social and racial justice. Since the Second Vatican Council there has been a profound change in the church's teaching and attitude to other religions. All these processes are ongoing and give hope for greater unity and

[69]Mark 10:44

co-operation between religions in the next millennium. However there is still much work to be done in bringing theology into line with these new approaches. It is also true that many Christian groups still put a great deal of effort into converting people of other faiths, believing it to have been enjoined by Christ himself.

At the heart of peacemaking is nonviolence. If we are violent in any way, then peace will soon depart. Emotional violence, perhaps the most hidden form, is one of the greatest destroyers of peace in families and communities. People can treat each other with emotional violence without even being aware of it. In order to avoid all forms of emotional violence we need much self-knowledge and humility. If we are being violent towards our own selves in any way at all, we will not be able to avoid being violent towards others, no matter how hard we try.

In meditation there can be a danger of bypassing our own emotional states and even repressing them in order to create the spiritual peace we think that meditation is supposed to give us. When this happens meditation and life cease to interact, growth stagnates and the peace Christ promised will not be gained. John Cassian warns us to "beware the pernicious peace"[70] and St. Benedict in his Rule for monks warns against giving a false peace.[71] I think there can be both inner and outer false peace, both equally harmful. Sweeping conflict under the carpet causes outer false peace. Inner false peace comes when we do the same with potential inner conflicts and emotions.

[70]*The Conferences of John Cassian*
[71]*The Rule of St. Benedict*

Another aspect of peacemaking which Thich Nhat Hanh, one of this century's great peacemakers, so clearly explains, is that if we seek to make peace we cannot take sides.

The situation in the world is like this. People completely identify with one side, one ideology. To understand the suffering and the fear of a citizen of the Soviet Union, we have to become one with him or her. To do so is dangerous— both sides will suspect us. But if we don't do it, if we align ourselves with one side or the other, we will lose our chance to work for peace. Reconciliation is to understand both sides, to go to one side and describe the suffering being endured by the other side, and then go to the other side and describe the suffering being endured by the first side. Doing only that will be a great help for peace.[72]

If we take sides we are already in conflict no matter how much we may say we want peace. This is a very difficult notion to take on board because we are almost always trying to make peace from one side of a conflict or another. When one understands this then one sees how rare a true peacemaker is. It is also the case that peacemakers in this true sense are rarely popular. If you are not on any side, you usually end up being suspected and rejected by both sides, as happened to Thich Nhat Hanh himself during the Vietnam War. Because he refused to blame or take sides, other peace workers and organizations rejected him because they suspected him of being on the other side, if he would not be on their side. When one looks deeply into this its truth

[72]Thich Nhat Hanh, *Being Peace* (Rider, 1992), 70.

becomes apparent. Not to take sides requires a high degree of detachment, or poverty of spirit. It requires the kind of unconditional love that belongs to the Divine.

Taking a look at what Jesus said about peace in the light of these thoughts may prove enlightening. "Peace I leave with you; my peace I give unto you; not as the world giveth do I give unto you."[73] Then in contrast to this, "I came not to send peace, but the sword."[74] At first glance these two statements appear to be contradictory. This is only one of many occasions when the teachings of Jesus appear to contradict one another. These apparent contradictions require that we look for deeper meanings and do not settle for literal or superficial interpretations of the teaching of Jesus.

It seems clear in the light of what has been said so far, that the peace the world cannot give is a peace that lies beyond the pairs of opposites, beyond taking sides. This kind of peace may often bring the sword of division on the superficial level of relating and may lead to the persecution of the peacemaker.

Not taking sides does not imply that we do not stand by anything in particular. Rather I think it means that we stand for the Truth, as we know it from the perspective of a pure heart and a deeper level of consciousness. This means that we will be fully aware that wherever there is conflict both parties are confused and unpeaceful. In conflicts of any kind no one side has all the truth. Thus when we take sides we identify ourselves with the partial right held by that view

[73]John 14:27 DV
[74]Matt. 10:34

of the conflict. Then we fail to see and respond to the right that is present in the opposite view.

The understanding of Truth is also an important aspect of this Beatitude. His Holiness the Dalai Lama[75] has pointed out that Truth itself need not be perceived as one 'thing'. Even Ultimate Truth could be multifaceted. The Christian teaching on the Trinity itself can help us to understand this, even God is understood not as a monad, but a multifaceted relational being. It is when we think there is only one truth and only one right that we feel obliged to take sides.

Another way of looking at this issue is to see two aspects of Truth, ultimate truth and relative truth. Both are true in their own dimension. All conflict exists in the realm of relative truth and only when we have had some glimpse of ultimate truth will we be able to avoid taking sides in issues of relative truth. In ultimate truth the pairs of opposites are embraced because it is a nondual state which the thinking mind cannot grasp because it can only operate in relative truth.

Thus being a peacemaker requires that we have some familiarity with the realm of undivided consciousness that is experienced through meditation and contemplative prayer. This is why it is so vital that meditation becomes more widely taught today. It is the way to experience reality directly and therefore to become peacemakers and to communicate the peace that Jesus came to give. "Peace I leave with you; my peace I give unto you; not as the world giveth do I give unto you."[76] This gift he gave after the resurrection

[75]*The Good Heart: His Holiness the Dalai Lama Comments on the Gospels* (Rider, 1996).
[76]John 14:27 DV

when he was operating from the ultimate realm of being and thus could communicate this type of peace directly. As we have seen again and again Jesus intends that his followers should live as he lived and do as he did. Thus he intends us to be peacemakers, but first we have to learn to lose our lives in the conditioned realm before we can find them in the ultimate realm. Although this is finally achieved through physical death and resurrection, it also happens in the little deaths and resurrections that occur every time we let go of something or someone in the conditioned realm. We can only do this when we have touched the profound understanding that comes through contemplation, of the impermanent nature of all things.

How can conflicts be resolved without taking sides? A mediator can enable people to resolve a conflict only if s/he can be impartial about the right and wrong on *both* sides. This cannot be done if the mediator favors one side or the other. On the human level there is victory and defeat. One person says, "OK, you win" and gives way to the other. This happens in families as well as in wars. People also give in "for the sake of peace." Usually this type of resolution will not last long, and leaves residues of simmering anger in the person who "gave in," even if they did so consciously in the cause of peace. We only need to look at the two world wars of this century to see the disastrous consequences of peace treaties imposed after defeat, especially if they are harsh and punitive. Compromise is another common way of reaching peace, and most modern political treaties attempt to work on this basis. Both sides give up something, so no one is defeated and punished, but both give in to some degree. This is the best that can be on the relative plain of reality. True peace will be the fruit of compassion and mutual forgiveness. For this each side needs to be able to truly stand in the shoes of the other and acknowledge what wrong they themselves have done in the course of the conflict. Only when this happens will true peace be born and the causes of the conflict will be dissolved in compassion. This resolution too may involve compromise in terms of behavior or actions growing out of the peace, but when the motivation is true compassion and forgiveness then both sides freely give their gift to the peace and true reconciliation is likely to occur. For this to happen some measure of spiritual understanding and self-transcendence need to be present.

Another aspect of peacemaking is learning to live and work peacefully with people whom we dislike, or who appear to dislike us. This is something we all have to do at some time in our lives. It is useful here to call to mind the words of His Holiness the Dalai Lama at the John Main seminar in 1994, "Our enemies are our best spiritual teachers." The people we dislike, and even more those who appear to dislike us, show up those aspects of ourselves that need to grow. When we are relating to the people in our lives that we find most difficult, our unresolved psychological weaknesses and fears tend to be brought to the fore. It is in this sense that these relationships are important teachers for us if we approach them with an honest and open heart. This type of situation brings us face to face with levels of emotional neediness and insecurity in ourselves that must be acknowledged and accepted before they can be healed and a deeper maturity reached. In this type of relationship we can be brought to an awareness of repeating patterns of negative behavior triggered by these wounds. Meditation creates within us the awareness and the space to begin to notice these patterns in time to change them. This in itself may improve difficult relationships. The insight thus gained leads to forgiveness and compassion, which leads to reconciliation and forgiveness.

Often people we do not like carry our projections and have those qualities we least like in ourselves. This is a difficult situation to live with, but it is also the way in which people we dislike are our best teachers. Recognizing this teaches us that there are no "bad guys" and "good guys." We all have, as the Buddhists say, both good seeds and seeds of suffering in our hearts. Thus we are all capable of the worst atrocities. We do not know what we would do in the circumstances of someone whose deeds fill us with horror. A poem of Thich Nhat Hanh illustrates this. It shows how we are all one and therefore responsible for everything that goes on in our world. When we have understood this truth with our deepest being, then maybe we will be ready to do the work of peacemaking in our world.

Do not say that I'll depart tomorrow
Because even today I still arrive.
Look deeply I arrive in every second
To be a bud on a spring branch,
To be a tiny bird, with wings still fragile,
    learning to sing in my new nest,
To be a caterpillar in the heart of a flower,
To be a jewel hiding itself in a stone.

I still arrive, in order to laugh and to cry,
In order to fear and to hope,
The rhythm of my heart is the birth and death of all that are
    alive.   .   .   .
I am the 12–year-old girl, refugee on a small boat,

Who throws herself into the ocean after being
     raped by a sea pirate
And I am the pirate, my heart not yet capable
     of seeing and loving. . . .
My joy is like spring, so warm it makes
     flowers bloom in all walks of life.
My pain is like a river of tears, so full it
     fills up the four oceans.
Please call me by my true names,
So I can hear all my cries and all my laughs at once,
So I can see that my joy and my pain are one.

Please call me by my true names,
     so I can wake up,
And so the door of my heart can be left open,
The door of compassion.[77]

These reflections throw new light on the words of Jesus:
"Judge not, that you may not be judged."[78]

---

[77]*Being Peace*, 63–64.
[78]Matt. 7:1; Luke 6:37.

Reflection 1

Think of a conflict situation in which you have been involved either in the past or present. Place yourself in that situation in your imagination.

1. Observe your feelings and reactions. Write them down.
2. Try to stand in the place of the other party and observe their feelings and reactions as honestly as you can. Write them down.
3. Write down your point of view and position in the conflict. Be clear about what it is you are standing for.
4. Write down the point of view and position of the other party. Be clear also what they stand for.
5. Now list all possible solutions you can see to the conflict. Observe how the solutions you have listed fit the following descriptions.
   a) Victory/defeat
   b) Compromise
   c) Compassion, understanding and mutual forgiveness
6. Which if any of the solutions could be said to be those of a true peacemaker?
7. If the conflict is past, observe how it could have been resolved differently in order to learn for the future. If it is present, how will this exercise help you to work with it?

Reflection 2

Do this exercise preferably after a period of meditation when the mind is relatively calm and quiet.

Think of the person that you find most difficult, either because you do not like them or you are convinced they do not like you.

What are the qualities in them that you find most difficult? Write them down. E.g., they are controlling and I feel unfree when they are present.

Now look at your own response to this quality. E.g., It makes me fearful. Why? What does this bring up in me? Does it remind me of authority figures I have feared? Can I practice a different mode of response to this person and not act on the fear pattern it creates in me? Over time it is possible to change patterns in this way.

Repeat this exercise with as many qualities as necessary.

At the end of the exercise spend some time sitting quietly breathing compassion and forgiveness towards that person as best you can, always being aware of your own feelings and having compassion towards these as well. In this breathing unite your heart with that of Christ and know that his boundless forgiveness is already there for both of you.

Chapter 12

Blessed Are They Who Suffer Persecution in the Cause of Right; Theirs Is the Kingdom of Heaven

This is the Beatitude most open to misinterpretation. Its position as the last of the eight seems to imply that it is the most difficult and needs the others to make it possible. We only need to look at history to see what tragic consequences come from misunderstanding this teaching. Even today people are willing to lay down their lives in order to kill as many people as possible who do not subscribe to their beliefs, and think that they will be rewarded by God for their deeds!

This is the horror of mistaking thoughts, beliefs and dogmas for ultimate truth. As long as there is the belief that ideas and thoughts embody the reality they attempt to express, then they have a dangerous power and can lead people to maim, torture, and kill their fellow human beings. Once we recognize that ideas can never truly manifest Reality, but only point to it, then we can be much freer in our approach to them. Often ideas are clung to out of fear and the failure to realize that actually religious beliefs are only ideas. When this is suggested to many religious people they become angry and feel that the very foundation of their faith is being questioned. The realization of the relativity of ideas needs to dawn on all of us at some time in our lives if we are to reach spiritual maturity.

To be able to sit more loosely with our ideas and opinions we need to realize that there is another way of knowing, especially in the things of the spirit. It requires that we have some degree of understanding of the functioning of the mind. Meditation leads us into the realm of experience that is beyond thought. Once we begin to touch this level of consciousness, unity consciousness beyond thought, then our ideas have far less power over us and we can become much more tolerant in our attitudes to beliefs and ideas that are radically different from our own.

In the realm of religion ideas can be dangerous. The intellect and the quest for truth and knowledge are, of course, great gifts. They become harmful when ideas are mistaken for the Reality they represent. Then humanity tries to play God and act on his behalf! This approach makes God in our image and likeness and does not allow the Absolute to be infinite and beyond the grasp of the human mind. New ideas and the restating of old truths can also cause fear in those in authority. Change is always difficult and intellectual change is no exception. This is the fear that causes people and institutions to cling to ideas and so to power.

There are people in the churches today with deep questions about traditional beliefs and teachings that they do not express because their religious upbringing has taught them not to question. This fear may be caused by a false image of God, which is often given through poor religious education. It is important to enable people to think and explore their understanding of faith at more adult depth. No one can tell us what to believe, we need to explore deeply for ourselves and accept things on our own conviction.

The Buddha taught people not to accept anything merely because he said it, but to seek to verify it for themselves. Doubt is not necessarily a bad thing, it can be a virtue that sets people free to search for truth and self-discovery in a way which mere adherence to imposed beliefs and creeds can never do. After all Jesus said "know the truth, and the truth will make you free."[79] He did not say have the right beliefs or subscribe to my ideas and you will be free. As we have already seen there are two ways of knowing which were recognized by Jesus. The clearest example of this can be found in the words of Paul: 'know the love of Christ which surpasseth knowledge."[80] It is not possible to know something that is beyond knowledge unless there is more than one way of knowing.

Only one who has reached this understanding can be capable of laying down their life for truth, as they know it, not as they believe it. Speaking the truth in love is in fact worlds away from arguing for what we believe. We cannot speak Truth and Love in this sense until we have gone beyond the realm of duality created by ideas. All wars and conflicts spring from the realm of the ego holding on to its views, rights, beliefs, desires, etc. This can be a personal ego, a family ego or a national or racial ego.

Many are ready to suffer for what they believe, and many die and kill for these things. But this is surely not what

[79]John 8:32
[80]Eph. 3:19 DV

Jesus means by suffering persecution in the cause of right. The perfect place to look for a clear understanding of this Beatitude is the life and death of Jesus himself. He never compromised the truth even though he knew it would mean death in the end. He sees truth that goes beyond human justice and retribution. Should the woman taken in adultery be stoned? "He that is without sin among you, let him cast the first stone at her."[81] Thus as long as one clings to an idea based on thought and therefore on relative truth, one will be in danger of laying down one's life for ideas instead of reality.

Mahatma Gandhi, Martin Luther King Jr., and Archbishop Oscar Romero are three examples of people who have lived this Beatitude in this century. Simone Weil is another; her radical living of truth, as she saw it, caused her early death. One thing that all these have strikingly in common is that they acted rather than spoke. They lived the truth and acted justice in the face of injustice and oppression. Because they did this to a radical degree, as Jesus did, they ended up being killed by their enemies. They were killed because the way they lived and acted exposed the falsehood of those who opposed them. They spoke and acted truth and justice in the face of untruth and injustice. When our relationship to Truth and Reality moves beyond the realm of ideas, then we become capable of living in the Truth. We may often find that simply living in the Truth is very threatening to people living in the realm of ideas, fantasy or self-delusion.

We may have faced a tiny example of this ourselves in the

[81]John 8:7

reaction of our friends to the fact that we meditate or go to church or practice religion at all. How often do we prefer not to admit that we do these things because we fear the ridicule and criticism that it will bring from our friends? This may be a first step to living this Beatitude, not hiding the fact that we meditate etc and that it is important to us. How hard it is to say, "Excuse me, I am going to do my meditation now, and will rejoin you in half an hour." How many very good reasons we find for not doing this.

One way of exploring how we live this Beatitude is to look at how often we fail to say what we deeply believe out of fear of the reaction of others. Yet on the other hand how readily we join in heated discussions about opinions which are far less important to us than the truths we fear to own.

Thus to understand this teaching we need to be on a spiritual journey that is beginning to break down the walls of ego domination in our being. It is the ego that generates fear at all levels. The ego is fearful of losing control of self, others and God, thus it weaves a web of fear. When we begin to meditate or enter seriously into any process of seeking spiritual self-knowledge, then we begin to face that fear and break free from it. This is the process of becoming capable of understanding and living these teachings of Jesus.

Reflection

After a period of meditation take some time to reflect:

1. What are the things in my life that I am most reluctant to own up to in front of acquaintances or even friends? Write them down. Why do I not speak of them? Are they not gifts that are worth sharing?

2. When did I last have a heated discussion over an idea—religious, political, or other? What was the idea? How deeply do I hold to it and why? Why did I need to get heated in defense of it?

3. Think of times in my life when I have lived by my Truth no matter what the cost. What was the outcome of this action? How does it differ from the above?

4. Are there some beliefs of religion with which I struggle? Do I find it difficult to deal with doubt? If so, why? Look for fears and write them down and seek their source. Do they lie in fear of God, fear of rejection, or a fear I cannot label?

5. Have I ever questioned the religious beliefs with which I was brought up?

6. Conversely, is there any belief I have rejected that could have deeper meaning if I looked at it afresh?

7. Without doubt and questioning very little

growth is possible. Therefore, if we fear to doubt positively the way we understand spiritual teachings, we will find progress on the path of spiritual development difficult or even blocked. Even Paul said, "When I was a child . . . I thought like a child. But when I became a man, I put away the things of a child."[82] How many of my beliefs have remained as I learned them in school? What can I do about it?

[82]1 Cor 13:11

Chapter 13

Mindfulness

C oming to the end of a retreat based on these reflections the question arises as to how to carry this experience back into everyday life without losing the richness, depth and insights which have been discovered. All these meditations and reflections require a practice of mindfulness if they are to be ongoing. The reflection exercises in this book may have led you to new levels of awareness, as well as a fuller self-knowledge.

Now the question is how to ensure that these insights bear fruit in our daily lives. The key to this lies in the transference of the levels of awareness achieved in meditation to our ordinary working state. This, according to Buddhism, is the main purpose and fruit of meditation. This state of awareness is called "mindfulness." Teachings on mindfulness are present in one form or another in all traditions. The teaching on mindfulness in the Buddhist tradition is particularly clear and practical. In Christianity we speak of living in the presence of God. Perhaps we have thought this meant thinking of God all the time, which of course is impossible. No, it means being totally and fully present to whatever we are doing at each moment. Then we are in the now and God is only in the now, therefore we are living in the presence of God.

In order to practice being mindful we have to stay totally

present to ourselves and our environment all the time. For most of us this seems an impossible thing to do, but it is something that can and must be learned if we are to make real progress on the spiritual path. Meditation itself leads to some development of mindfulness, but the more conscious we are of the process and the more we work at it outside our periods of meditation, the sooner it will be developed.

Here is a quote from the Buddha's words on mindfulness from the *Satipatthana-sutta*:

> This is the only way, Bikkhus, for the purification of beings, for the overcoming of sorrow and lamentations, for the destruction of suffering and grief, for reaching the right path, for the attainment if Nibbana, namely the four foundations of mindfulness. What are the four?
>
> Here a Bikkhu, ardent, clearly comprehending things and mindful, lives observing the activities of the body, having overcome covetousness and repugnance towards the world of body; observing feelings, having overcome covetousness or repugnance towards the world of feeling. . . . Observing activities of the mind, having overcome covetousness and repugnance towards the world of mind; observing mental objects, having overcome covetousness and repugnance towards the world of mental objects.[83]

This quote shows the level of attention needed to all aspects of our being in order to be fully present. The Sutra goes on to explain in detail the path of awareness in meditation and outside it. In Buddhism the practice of mindful-

---

[83]An abridged quote from the *Satipatthana-sutta*, in Walpola Rahula, *What the Buddha Taught* (Gordon Fraser, 1985), 109–110.

ness starts with breath awareness and body awareness. In this form of meditation we simply watch the breath. When we do this even for a short time we notice how much there is to notice about the breath. Watch the length, depth, quality, and speed of the breath and how these vary according to the state of our mind. Instruction on this can be found in the Satipatthana-sutta.[84] Following this comes mindfulness of the body. Just watching the sensations in the body can be a revelation! There is so much more going on in terms of sensations, itches, little aches, etc., than we are aware of most of the time.

The Buddha recommended four postures for meditation: sitting, walking, standing and lying down. We spend our whole lives in one or other of these postures or moving between them; thus it is clear that mindfulness is meant as a full meditation in daily living.

Usually, we are not fully present to what we are doing because even when we are working, our thoughts and feelings are engaged in the past and the future. The more we are engaged by past fears or future expectations, the less we will be able to be mindful in the present. This is why it is important to face some of the issues dealt with in previous chapters and to work through them so that we can be ready and able to practice mindfulness of the present moment.

It is easy to be present to tasks that absorb our whole attention. Such tasks as painting, calligraphy, or mathematics fall into this category. However often in this case we lose awareness as well. Both awareness of self and of the task are

---

[84]Sattipattana-sutta, *The Foundation of Mindfulness Sutra,* in *The Buddha and His Teachings* by Narada Maha Thera.

needed for full mindfulness. Self-awareness in this context is not self-consciousness, but a free flowing awareness of the performance of each movement or action, without the presence of the judgmental ego sense.

Mindfulness of walking in the Buddha's teaching is the first step or the link between mindfulness in meditation and in everyday life. This can be practiced on the many occasions when we have to walk somewhere. Instead of letting the mind run ahead or behind as it normally would we pay close attention to the act of walking: watching how the feet move, how we breathe when walking, what muscles are used, etc., and simply being with the feet on the ground and the breath. When we reach our destination, whatever we had to do there will be much better accomplished for having walked there mindfully. Very often the thoughts we have about a task as we walk towards it are not helpful to its performance and on many occasions may be harmful. Rehearsing what we think will happen distorts our perception of what actually happens when we get there. Then we respond to our perception and not the reality. Thus mindful walking towards action can lead into mindful action as well.

Being mindful while standing can be very practical also. How often do we have to stand and wait for things: for buses, in the line at the post office or ticket office, etc. Instead of daydreaming or feeling impatient, the practice of mindfulness can be very fruitful. Paying attention to our own bodies and minds first of all and then to the activity going on around us could well lead to feelings of compassion for others arising.

Lying down, again before sleep or on waking, attention to what is happening in our body and mind can prepare either for a good night's sleep or lead us positively into a new day. Thus at every moment, especially moments when the mind could wander off on its own agenda, mindfulness helps to keep us aware and also to avoid negative thoughts arising in the mind. It is the primary way of ensuring that our minds work for us but do not control us and set the agenda though uncontrolled reverie.

Making a general resolution to be mindful will not help, this is impossible, and therefore will soon be forgotten. The best way to begin to encourage mindfulness is to take moments of our day when we are alone and doing fairly mundane actions. Try performing these actions with full awareness and total concentration. At first, it may be helpful to simply talk oneself through the action. For example in making a cup of tea: "filling the kettle, turning off the tap, plugging in kettle, taking cup, opening tea . . . etc." Avoid using the personal pronoun "I" so that attention is held on the performing of the action, rather than on the ego and its responses. However, this does not exclude being aware of one's states, in this case anticipation of enjoying the tea, or being tired and needing a lift and so on. The use of this practice helps us to grow more and more in living in the presence of God that is only available to us when we are present in the moment.

It is easier to be mindful and present when we are alone in silence. When we are with others it is much more difficult. Often we find ourselves preparing our answer to what someone is saying instead of giving our whole being and attention to listening to what they are saying, in their words and also behind their words. This is the most difficult type of mindfulness of all. Yet, people sense at once if we are really hearing them or not. When we are interacting with others, the ego is at its busiest. To become aware of the thoughts and feelings generated by these moments and to simply smile and let them go is a first and important step in becoming more mindful in relationships. In this way we begin to catch our negative behavior patterns before they spring into action and can simply let them pass without being activated. This is one of the most important fruits of mindfulness.

Living this way becomes a source of great peace and joy. It enables us to experience the Happiness that Jesus speaks of in the Beatitudes. When we learn to experience happiness in the here and now we are able to share it with all the people in our lives.

Reflection

1. Make a list of what you see as the most important insights you have gained from these reflections.
2. Think of things that will help you keep them in mind as you move on.
3. In what ways and places do you want to try to practice mindfulness?
4. Think of ways of ensuring some time and space in your life for ongoing reflection and practice.
5. Read again the reflections for chapters 1 and 3 and see what things might have changed for you.

Conclusion

It is my hope that this journey will have opened new windows for you in several directions, not least to the wonders of the Gospels and the riches they hold. Today there is so much renewal in various areas of Christian life. It is important that we let go of our past prejudices regarding our own tradition and come to look at it with fresh eyes, free from the wounds of the past.

As Christians we are a community of the disciples of Christ, all wounded, but all also whole and made in the image of God. We are the Body of Christ in the world today and in learning to live out his teaching contained in the Beatitudes we can become channels for his unconditional love and wisdom to flow afresh in our own communities and beyond them. Love of Christ and our own tradition needs to be a liberating love that enables us to love and see the beauty in other traditions as the Vatican Council suggested we should. Faith in God through Christ is not about beliefs or rules, it is about the power of the Spirit working within each one. Finding our own true beliefs is a part of maturing in faith. This process comes from deep reflection on Scripture, and as we have seen, can be enhanced by reading them in the light of other faiths.

The Church needs to be seen as a community of the disciples of Jesus. This community has many spiritual families within it, where we can feel at home according to our inclinations. It is a mistake to identify the Church with the institutions it has developed, and even worse to identify Christ and his life in the world today with institutions, instead of with communities. Christ can never be limited to the church. He is surely speaking to us from many directions today and perhaps not least through the advent of Buddhism in the West. Could he be calling us back to a new understanding of our faith through this? Perhaps this book goes a little way in showing how this might be the case.

Appendix

AN OVERVIEW OF BUDDHISM

One of the reasons Buddhism is growing so fast in the West is because of its practical and nondogmatic nature. The Buddha's basic teaching is that life in this world is unsatisfactory and contains much suffering, but that there is a way out of this dilemma. This is what people today are seeking. Material wealth and technological advances have not proved to be the panacea they were expected to be at the turn of this century. In many ways Western institutional religion has also failed to provide people with practical answers to the dilemmas of this age. Hence many, especially the young, are turning to the various forms of Buddhism present in the West today. What then is the Buddha's solution?

First a brief sketch of the life of the Buddha. The word 'buddha' means awakened one. The Buddha's name was Siddharta Gautama; he was a prince of the Sakya clan living in north India around 500 B.C.E. Seeing the reality of old age, sickness and death, he left his wealth and luxury and became a wandering sage, seeking an answer to these suffering situations of human existence. After learning all he could from other wandering sages he realized that neither the extremes of indulgence or asceticism could provide the answer. Then, the story goes, he sat down under a tree and vowed not to rise until he had found the answer. During the night that ensued he was tempted by Mara (the Buddhist Satan) and as dawn broke he achieved enlightenment. He saw the answer to suffering. At first reluctant, when requested by the gods, he agreed to teach others, because as the god pointed out to him, there were those with only a little dust in their eyes who were ready to hear the teaching. And so he began to turn the wheel of dharma (teaching). He taught for forty years, before passing into Nirvana at the age of around eighty.

The foundation of the Buddha's teaching, which is common to all schools of Buddhism, is the Four Noble Truths and dependent origination. These teachings encapsulate the insight into the nature of the world that the Buddha had on the night of his enlightenment. What the Buddha awoke to was an understanding of the nature of suffering, how to overcome it in this life, and so break the cycle of birth and death to which all beings are subject (*samsara*).

The Buddha never required people to accept his teaching on his word, but he encouraged them to test it for themselves and if it worked accept it, if not, to leave it aside. Many people find this approach refreshing and attractive. There is a profound difference between belief and experience, reason and heart knowledge. Since the time of the so-called Enlightenment, the age of reason, heart knowledge and experience have often been devalued and neglected in the West and Christianity has shared the disastrous consequences of this. As in all things, the middle way is important. As all the great teachers show, experience never denies reason, but builds on and transcends it.

The Four Noble Truths are:

1. The truth of suffering, or unsatisfactoriness: The term used here is *dukkha*. It is a word difficult to translate. Suffering is an inadequate translation and has led many to believe Buddhism has a negative view of life. Rather this truth indicates that there is no perfection in this world because all is impermanent, we know that nothing we gain can last forever. This reality takes complete happiness from us and causes fear.

2. The cause of suffering: This truth indicates that people suffer because of desire and aversion. Either we cling to the things we want or hanker after them if we do not have them; or we push away what we do not want or fear it if we do not have it. The assumption behind this grasping and aversion is that things are permanent.

3. The cessation of suffering: This comes about when we learn not to cling to or resist impermanence as if it were permanent.

4. The way to the cessation of suffering is the Noble Eightfold Path.

In Buddhist terms trying to make the impermanent permanent is the root cause of human unhappiness. The fact is recognized that this situation can cease even in this lifetime when we have fully understood the meaning of impermanence, not merely in our minds but in our whole being. The Noble Eightfold Path is the way to bring this understanding into all aspects of our lives. The statements of Jesus, "know the truth, and the truth shall make you free,"[85] and "He that

[85]John 8:32

shall lose his life for my sake, shall save it"[86] reflect similar ideas.

This law of impermanence is called the law of dependent origination. This implies that nothing in this world exists of and by itself. All things depend on the causes and conditions that allow them to come into being. Everything is dependent for its existence on other things. It is not hard to see the truth of this for oneself intellectually. We too are not isolated self-sufficient entities, but the result of a vast network of causes and conditions. Seeing this we can see that we too are impermanent. Not only are all things dependent on causes and conditions, they are made up of many parts, yet a thing or person cannot be identified by any individual part, nor is it merely the sum of its parts. This means that things as we see them have no real or self-existent nature. The complete understanding of this fact is said to liberate us from clinging or aversion whether for ourselves, or others, or things in this world

This leads to the Buddhist concept of *anatta* or not-self, which is probably the most misunderstood concept in all Buddhism. It does not mean that we are not real or that we do not have a self. It means that we are not a fixed, permanent, unchanging, self-sufficient entity independent of others. It is easy to see that this is true, yet we act all the time as if we were a separate independent being. This is the ego's great delusion, which the teachings of the Buddha set out to destroy.

The Buddhist system of philosophy is vast and much of it revolves around this teaching. Nagarjuna, a great Indian

[86]Luke 9:24 DV

Buddhist philosopher, who lived around 200 C.E., developed the deepest thinking around this subject, known as *Madhyamaka*. He developed the philosophy of emptiness or *Sunyata*. This posits that absolutely everything in this universe, right up to the highest beings and even pure awareness itself is empty of self-existence. Thus absolutely everything is dependently originated. Emptiness on the other hand is the void from which all emerges.

The Noble Eightfold Path is the summary of the Buddha's teaching on the way to end *dukkha*, suffering, unsatifactoriness. This way out does not remove pain or old age or death, it removes the suffering we create for ourselves by reacting wrongly to the circumstances of life in this world.

1. Right view.[87] View here needs to be understood as perception. It is the foundation for all spiritual practice. It implies the capacity to see the world and life and ourselves as they really are. In Buddhist terms this implies at least an intellectual understanding of the Four Noble Truths, dependent origination and not-self. Without this basic understanding we are living in a state of illusion. On the other hand of course spiritual practice enables right view and deepens it until this view of reality changes our whole way of being. It can be seen as the ability to distinquish the permanent from the inpermanent.

2. Right intention. In Buddhism intention is very important because karma depends on intention. Basically to

---

[87]The word *right* in these statements should not be taken as moral right as versus wrong so much as simply the true or correct way of looking at things.

have right intention implies the desire to do good rather than harm to other sentient beings, not only human beings.

3. Right speech. As in every religion, the Buddha recognized the potential of the tongue to do harm. Therefore all forms of false speech, gossip, or hurtful speech are to be avoided. This is because basically they spring from a deluded version of whom we are in relation to others.

4. Right action. This usually follows right intention, but we know it is possible to act wrongly from right intention. Again, here right action implies living and acting in accordance with the basic principle of nonharming.

5. Right livelihood. This is interesting because it has no direct equivalent in Christian thinking as far as I know. It means that one should earn one's living only in ways that do no harm to self, other sentient beings, and the planet. Thus anything to do with the production of arms would be considered wrong livelihood; so would being a butcher! This is a concept that gives much food for thought in today's world.

6. Right effort. This too is an interesting concept. It implies there is wrong or unhelpful effort. This is often applied to meditation, but equally applies to all form of effort. Effort to force change in an unnatural or over-hasty manner would be seen as wrong effort. It usually defeats the purpose and produces results other than those hoped for.

7. Right mindfulness. It is difficult to see how there could be wrong mindfulness, so I assume this to mean that we should be mindful. This means being fully present to ourselves and to all that is going on around us. This has been fully dealt with in chapter 13 of this book.

8. Right samadhi. This is a difficult word to translate. It can be rendered as concentration or contemplation. This

latter sense appears truer to the essential meaning. It is a state of deep awareness and focused presence. In Buddhism there are many degrees of samadhi and it can appear very technical. Basically for our purposes here it can be taken to mean the deepest states of meditation. These are often understood today as altered states of consciousness. This is because when we are in these deep states we produce brain wave patterns unique to them. It is this latter factor which is leading to much scientific research into the effects and fruits of meditation, or being in these deeper states on a regular basis. Through the levels of samadhi we come to experience the non-dual reality behind the illusion of duality.

Central to Buddhism as to all Eastern religions is the concept of reincarnation. There are many views on this and it is a very popular, but much misused idea by people in the West today. It is inseparable from the concept of karma, which is part of the law of causality. It is karma that propels consciousness from life to life. Even within the different schools of Buddhism the understanding of these ideas and their relationship varies. For our purposes here it is sufficient to say that our consciousness is seen not to have begun at birth or to end at death. Rather we come into this world bearing the imprints on our consciousness of the actions of past lives. This is referred to as karma, good and bad, and which works itself out in this lifetime, during which we accumulate more to carry us into the next life. Karma is part of the theory of dependent origination. It is only when we have freed ourselves from the effects of all our karma and ceased to accumulate any more, good or bad, that we are finally liberated from the wheel of birth and death. This state is seen as *Nir-*

vana and/or the state of enlightenment. It is possible to achieve this state while still living in this world, as the Buddha himself did. This in fact is the meaning of the word *buddha*.

To see these ideas in context we need to have some basic idea of Buddhist cosmology. This is vast and very different from the limited understanding of the cosmos on which the biblical myths of creation were founded. The wheel of time and birth and death is beginningless. In beginningless time worlds, universes, solar systems are born and die, but the realm of cyclic existence rolls on. Within this endless flow there are many realms, of which the material realm that we are familiar with is but one. The human realm is seen as very important because within this realm we shape our future destiny; in other realms we only suffer or enjoy the consequences of our actions here. There are heavenly realms and hellish realms and hungry ghosts and animals. These are all realms into which we can be reborn according to our karma. Except for the animal realm, time is very different from this present realm. However it is important to remember that both heaven and hell realms are temporary, they are not our final destiny. This lies beyond the wheel of time. Within these realms there also exist other types of beings, *devas* (probably closest to angels, though usually translated as gods) and demons of various types. Hungry ghosts are spirits full of desire and attachment that is never satisfied.

The state beyond the wheel of time is spoken of as the realm of the Deathless or Nirvana. This is because all that the Buddha said about it is that there is the unborn, the undying, and the uncreated.

Historically Buddhism has divided into two major

streams. The Mahayana ("great vehicle") and the Hinayana ("lesser vehicle"), today mostly referred to as Theravada because Hinayana has been used as a derogatory term. Theravada Buddhism exists today mainly in the South: Sri Lanka, Burma, Thailand, and Cambodia. The Mahayana spread from India to China, Japan, Mongolia, and Tibet. Within the Mahayana is the Vajrayana also known as the Tantrayana; this latter is today mainly associated with Tibetan Buddhism.

Theravada Buddhism only recognizes the Pali Canon as authentic teachings of the Buddha. This is the large body of Sutras, Vinaya and Abhidharma literature that exists in the Pali language. Vipassana, insight meditation, and mindfulness are the main teachings associated with this school in the West today.

The Mahayana on the other hand accepts a whole body of Sutras which the Buddha is said to have taught from a higher plane and only revealed to those who were ready to receive them and who would reveal them when the time was right. The Mahayana includes all Zen, Tibetan and Pure Land schools of Buddhism.

This basic split is supposed to have occurred within 300 years of the Buddha's death. Here I am trying to give a brief outline of a very complex process.[88] The two main causes appear to have been the development of an overly monastic system, which left little hope for the laity on the one hand, and what some saw as an overly personalized view of enlightenment. This led within the Mahayana to the development

---

[88]This history is no less complex than the splits within Christianity, though generally much less violent.

of a much more important role for the lay community, and more importantly from our perspective, the development of the Bodhisattva ideal.

The Bodhisattva is one who reaches the very highest state, just short of enlightenment, but then chooses not to enter the fully enlightened state and so move beyond the realm of time, but to remain and work for others until all sentient beings are saved. This is understood to be the ultimate unselfish act towards which all should aspire. Hence ordinary people take the Bodhisattva vow even though they know they are yet far from being Bodhisattvas. Thus this goal in the Mahayana has in many ways become more important than enlightenment itself. Just to desire enlightenment for oneself is viewed as selfish. This is where the basic criticism of the Hinayana lies, in that its followers are said to seek only their own enlightenment. Though these days this need not be true; there is much unselfish work for others being done within the Theravada scene.

Morality in Buddhism is seen within the context of dependent origination. We are all interconnected with all beings and the planet, therefore it is in our best interests to respect to the utmost the web of life on which our survival depends. From this perspective one could say that the sole moral tenet in Buddhism is to live without harming anything in this web of life. Clearly to do this fully we need a highly developed understanding of this teaching. But this one tenet actually covers every aspect of our life. Just as in the matter of teaching, there are no moral dogmas; one is expected to work things out according to this understanding. That is not to say that in Buddhist countries customs and taboos do not abound. They do, as does a good deal of superstition, as in all religions, but these are not in the teaching as such.

How does one become a Buddhist? There is one simple way and that is to take refuge in the Three Jewels: the Buddha, the Dharma, and the Sangha. These are known as "the refuges" and are the foundation of all schools. The Buddha does not only mean Siddharta Gautama the historical Buddha, but also the buddha-nature or enlightened mind, which is in every sentient being waiting to be revealed. The Dharma also can be seen on two levels. The Dharma is the teaching of the Buddha at one level, but also the true law, ground of being, the way things really are. The Sangha is the community of those who practice the Dharma, which at one level can be seen as the monastic community, or all higher beings, or just the local group of practitioners with whom I associate. The Mahayana extends these three into the three bodies of the Buddha, the Dharmakaya, ground of all being, the Sambhogakaya, a difficult concept referring to the spirit body, or all higher beings, Bodhisattva's realm, and the Nirmanakaya, which is the realm of manifestation here. Thus when the Buddha lived on earth he was in his Nirmanakaya body.

The two great virtues in Buddhism are Wisdom and Compassion. They are essential and both are necessary for progress on the path. In the Mahayana they are personified in the two great Bodhisattvas, Avalokiteshvara (Chenresig in Tibetan)—Compassion and Manjushri (Wisdom). Many Tibetans see His Holiness the Dalai Lama as an incarnation of Chenresig.

This I hope will give those readers new to Buddhism sufficient understanding to enable them to relate to the subjects discussed in the chapters of this book. It may also stimulate you to explore these topics further and to see other ways in which they help you to make sense of your own faith in the modern world.

Glossary

Abbreviations: S = Sanskrit ; P = Pali

Abhishiktananda (S): Indian name of Henri le Saux. Meaning Bliss of the Anointed.

Advaita (S): Nonduality; Not one, not two.

Anatta (P): No-Self; having no independent self-existent identity.

Arunachala: Holy mountain in Tamil Nadu, South India near the town of Tiruvannamalai.

Bikkhu (P): Buddhist monk; meaning "venerable sir."

Dukkha (P): Suffering; unsatisfactoriness; insubstantiality.

Dharma (S) Dhamma (P): The teaching of the Buddha; also Truth, righteousness, nature, all things and states conditioned and unconditioned.

Hinayana (S): Lit., the lesser vehicle; A term given to a particular category of practice in which refuge is taken only in the scriptures revealed during the Buddha's life and known as the Tipitaka (P) "three baskets" of teachings containing the Sutras, the Vinaya and the Abhidharma. They are also called the Pali Canon. Today the Hinayana is mainly found in southern countries of Sri Lanka, Burma, Thailand and Cambodia. It is also known as Theravada Buddhism. This path consists mainly in the trainings in morality (Sila), concentration (Samatha) and wisdom or insight (Vipassana).

Karma (S) Kamma (P): Lit., action or deed. It is most often used to denote the process of physio-psychic evolution, which is controlled by actions of body speech and mind. According to the laws of karma, no experience is causeless; rather, everything that occurs has its seed in a previous action, and every action sows its seed on the mind, which will eventually ripen in accordance with its nature. In brief an evil deed produces the seed of future suffering, and goodness produces the seed of happiness. Technically, karma is of two main types. The latter refers to a deed done with awareness of emptiness; this produces no effect on the doer. Contaminated karmas are bad, good and steady, resulting in lower rebirth, good rebirth, and rebirth in the realm of form respectively.

Madhyamaka (S): School of Buddhist philosophy of which Nagarjuna is the most famous exponent. It is the most radical teaching on the emptiness of all phenomena and is the teaching that is used by His Holiness the Dalai Lama and many Tibetan teachers.

Mahayana (S): Lit., the great vehicle; the vehicle in which refuge is taken in the scriptures revealed after the Buddha's death that were propagated by masters such as Nagarjuna and Asanga, as well as in the earlier scriptures accepted by the Hinayana. Also unlike the Hinayana, whose basis is renunciation, the basis of the Mahayana is great compassion; and its aim, rather than personal Nirvana, is fully omniscient buddhahood.

Mantra (S): Sacred syllables recited for their spiritually transformative power. Now taken commonly to mean sacred word or sound recited or sung as a form of prayer. Mantras are a very important part of Tibetan Tantric Buddhism.

Maranatha (Aramaic): "Come, Lord" or "the Lord comes."

Nirvana (S) **Nibbana** (P): Lit., blowing out. Usually refers to the ultimate state to be attained in Buddhism. Liberation from cyclic existence.

Paticca-samuppada (P): dependent origination; conditioned genesis; nothing is self- existent all things depend for their existence on prior causes and conditions.

Samadhi (S): Meditative powers of mind. As a mental faculty, samadhi is the ability to concentrate one-pointedly. In meditation, samadhi becomes the ability to totally absorb the mind in an object of concentration.

Samatha (S): Tranquillity; concentration; usually refers to meditation practice to develop these qualities.

Samsara (S): Cyclic existence; characterized for humans by birth, old age, sickness and death.

Sangha (S): Conventionally the community of ordained Buddhist monks; however this is often broadened to include the whole community of spiritual aspirants. Ultimately, the Sangha are those with direct experience of ultimate reality. These are the High Ones.

Sunyata (P): Emptiness; having no independent existence. This however is not nihilism.

Tantra (S): A class of esoteric teachings and practices in Mahayana Buddhism, also referred to as the Vajrayana path. There are also Hindu Tantras.

Theravada (S): See Hinayana.

Vajrayana (S): "the diamond vehicle" Tibetan Tantric way.

Vedanta (S): Lit., the end of the Vedas, refers to the Upanishadic era of Hinduism. It is also the word used to refer to the Hindu advaitic tradition.

Vipassana (P): Insight meditation in Theravada Buddhism.

Further Reading

Interfaith

The Good Heart. Robert Kiely, ed. Wisdom.

The Ground We Share. David Steindl-Rast and Aitkin Roshi. Triumph Books.

Hindu Christian Meeting Point. Abhishiktananda. ISPCK.

The Secret of Arunachala Abhishiktananda. ISPCK.

The Marriage of East and West. Bede Griffiths. DLT.

A New Vision of Reality. Bede Grifiths. DLT.

The Hidden Christ of Hinduism. Raimon Pannikar. DLT.

Transcendence Daniel Faivre, ed., available from the editor at: 2 Church Ave., Southall Middx, UB2 4BL, England.

The Long Search. Ninian Smart. BBC.

Saccidananda: An Advaitic View of the Trinity. Abhishiktananda. ISPCK.

Religions in Conversation. Michael Barnes. Abingdon Press, 1989.

Christian Uniqueness Reconsidered. Gavin D'Costa. Orbis, 1990

The Myth of Christian Uniqueness. John Hick and Paul Knitter. Orbis, 1987.

Meditation (Christian Tradition)

Word into Silence. John Main, OSB. DLT.

The Inner Christ. John Main, OSB. DLT.

Christian Meditation: Your Daily Practice. Laurence Freeman, OSB. Medio Media.

Light Within. Laurence Freeman, OSB. DLT.

The Selfless Self. Laurence Freeman, OSB. DLT

The New Creation in Christ. Bede Griffiths. DLT.

Prayer. Abhishiktananda. ISPCK.

Silent Music. William Johnston, SJ.

Mirror Mind. William Johnston, SJ.

Silent Wisdom, Hidden Light. Eileen O'Hea. Medio Media and Arthur James.

Lost Christianity. Jacob Needleman. Element Classic Series, 1993.

The Practice of Zen Meditation. Hugo M. Enomiya-Lassalle, SJ. Acquarian 1987

Buddhism

What the Buddha Taught. Walpola Rahula. Gordon Fraser, 1985. (Theravada)

The Tibetan Book of Living and Dying. Sogyal Rinpoche Rider. (Tibetan Buddhism)

A Path with Heart. Jack Kornfield. Rider.

Boundless Heart. Alan Wallace, Zara Houshmand, ed. Snow Lion, 1999.

A Passage from Solitude. B. Alan Wallace. Snow Lion, 1992.

No Boundary. Ken Wilber. Shambala.

One Taste. Ken Wilber. Shambala, 1999. (And any other of his many books)

Old Path White Clouds, Walking in the Footsteps of the Buddha. Thich Nhat Hanh. Parallax Press, 1991.

Publications produced by Amaravati Buddhist Monastery for free distribution can be obtained from: Amaravati Bud-

dhist Monastery, Gt. Gaddesden, Hemel Hempsted, UK.
The following are specially recommended:

Cittaviveka. Ajahn Sumedho.

The Way It Is. Ajahn Sumedho.

About the Author

Elizabeth West was born in Birmingham, England in 1944; she spent most of her childhood and youth in southern Africa. She became a Roman Catholic nun at the age of eighteen. After returning to the U.K. she qualified as a teacher. Her interest in Eastern religions began in 1977 with the experience of a yoga and meditation retreat led by two Catholic nuns from India. She then spent time in India in Hindu and Christian ashrams. After taking an M.A. in World Religions at London University she worked for six years with the Westminster Roman Catholic Diocese Interfaith Programme. During this time she made retreats led by Buddhist teachers of both the Theravada and Zen traditions. Leaving her religious order, she joined the Christian Meditation Community in 1992. Through her work with this community her interest in Buddhism was enhanced by the experience of the dialogues with His Holiness the Dalai Lama. On several occasions she has led Buddhist/Christian retreats with various Buddhist teachers. This book has been inspired by the experience of the dialogues that took place within these retreats.

The World Community for Christian Meditation

Meditation creates community. Since the first Christian Meditation Centre was started by John Main in 1975, a steadily growing community of Christian meditators has spread around the world.

The International Centre in London co-ordinates this world-wide community of meditators. A quarterly newsletter, giving spiritual teaching and reflection, is sent out from London and distributed from a number of national centers, together with local and international news of retreats and other events being held in the world-wide community. An annual John Main Seminar is held.

The International Centre is funded entirely by donations and especially through a Friends of the International Centre programme.

The World Community for Christian Meditation / International Centre / 23 Kensington Square / London W8 5HN / United Kingdom.   Tel: +44 171 937 4679   Fax: +44 171 937 6790 E-mail: wccm@compuserve.com

Web Page

Visit The World Community for Christian Meditation Web site for information, weekly meditation group readings, and discussion at: www.wccm.org

Christian Meditation Centre / 1080 West Irving Park Rd / Roselle IL 60172. Tel/Fax: +1 630 351 2613

John Main Institute / 7315 Brookville Rd. / Chevy Chase / MD 20815. Tel: +1 301 652 8635 E-Mail: wmcoerp@erols.com

Christian Meditation Centre / 1619 Wight St. / Wall / NJ 07719. Tel: +1 732 681 6238 Fax: +1 732 280 5999 E-mail: gjryan@aol.com

Christian Meditation Center / 193 Wilton Road West / Ridgefield / CT 06877. Tel: +1 203 438 2440 E-mail: Internet:pgulick@mci2000.com

The Cornerstone Centre / 1215 East Missouri Ave. / Suite A 100 / Phoenix / AZ 85014-2914. Tel: +1 602 279 3454 Fax: +1 602 957 3467 E-mail: ecrmjr@woddnet.attnet

Medio Media Ltd.

Medio Media Ltd. is the publishing arm of the World Community for Christian Meditation.

A catalogue of Medio Media's publications—books, audio sets, and videos—is available from:

Medio Media / 15930 N. Oracle Road # 196 / Tucson / AZ 85739. Tel: +1 800 324 8305 Fax: +1 520 818 2539 Web page: www.mediomedia.com